I0542882

PERSONAL FINANCE FOR TEENS

MASTER BUDGETING, SAVING, AND INVESTING
THROUGH HANDS-ON, ENGAGING, AND TEEN-
FRIENDLY ACTIVITIES TO EMPOWER FINANCIAL
LITERACY AND DECISION-MAKING

J.R. ORR

© **Copyright 2023 - All rights reserved.**

The content contained within this book may not be reproduced, duplicated or transmitted without direct written permission from the author or the publisher.

Under no circumstances will any blame or legal responsibility be held against the publisher, or author, for any damages, reparation, or monetary loss due to the information contained within this book, either directly or indirectly.

Legal Notice:

This book is copyright protected. It is only for personal use. You cannot amend, distribute, sell, use, quote, or paraphrase any part of the content within this book without the consent of the author or publisher.

Disclaimer Notice:

Please note that the information contained within this document is for educational and entertainment purposes only. All effort has been made to present accurate, up-to-date, reliable, and complete information. No warranties of any kind are declared or implied. Readers acknowledge that the author is not engaged in the rendering of legal, financial, medical, or professional advice. The content within this book has been derived from various sources. Please consult a licensed professional before attempting any techniques outlined in this book.

By reading this document, the reader agrees that under no circumstances is the author responsible for any losses, direct or indirect, that are incurred as a result of the use of the information contained within this document, including, but not limited to, errors, omissions, or inaccuracies.

CONTENTS

INTRODUCTION

Finances. Even the word sounds daunting. Thinking about finances can just run a montage of numbers and statistics in your mind. It's no wonder that so many teenagers don't know anything about finances and don't think they can ask anyone for help. It's definitely a more common problem than you might think. If you feel confused when it comes to money and finances, you are definitely not alone.

I could tell you hundreds of stories of young people and teenagers who have struggled with finances but were able to turn it around. One of these people is Jonathan, and he was just 16 years old when he decided he needed to learn about finances. He didn't really have any knowledge of what it was, but he kept reading that it all starts with saving. So he decided that's what he was going to do. He only had enough to save about $15 every month, and it seemed pointless, but he did it anyway. After about a year and a half, he saw his savings grow to about $1,000. It was because he learned how to save and where to put his money. A year after that, it almost doubled, and he was completely shocked. He realized that it really was that simple, and the principles for handling your finances don't have to be complicated.

This is just one story, and there are hundreds of other stories about teenagers starting businesses, learning to save, spending more wisely, and setting foundational financial goals. If you think you're too young to get started with finances, you are definitely mistaken. It doesn't matter your age; in fact, the younger you are, the better it's going to be. You are in such a crucial position in your life because you can learn how to handle your finances in a safe space where you don't have a ton of financial pressure on you. When you do grow up and have a steady stream of income, you already have the basic building blocks for financial success. This is why starting now is so crucial.

By the time you close this book, you will have all the knowledge you need to make better financial decisions and manage your money well. You will be able to narrow down your financial goals so you have something to work towards. Learning to budget and handling your money with less stress and anxiety are skills that come along with all the knowledge in this book. This is what you can take into your future and your life as you grow older. Once the habits are built, it becomes a lot easier for you to manage this area of your life.

If you are struggling to understand finances or you just want to get a kickstart on managing them, then this is the right book for you. It doesn't matter how much money you're starting out with; even if that number is zero, you can start planning and managing your finances today. In the future, you will be so thankful that you took the steps to become better with your money. The first thing that you need to understand about money is how to budget. That is exactly what we are going to be covering in the next chapter, so buckle in and let's go!

1

YOUR MONEY, YOUR PLAN: A BUDGET THAT WORKS FOR YOU

There is nothing better than pulling through a drive-thru and getting your favorite coffee order. If you aren't a coffee drinker, Starbucks and other coffeehouses have tons of other options available —but this comes at a price. Gen Z is taking on the same coffee culture as their predecessors, the Millennials. Coffee seems to be a huge expense for people 35 and younger. In fact, one study showed that 41% of Millennials spend more on coffee than they save in their retirement accounts (Housman, 2020).

Wendy would probably fall into those statistics because she loved her Starbucks blended strawberry lemonade drink. She had recently just gotten her driver's license, and whenever she could, she would pull into the Starbucks drive-through and buy a delicious drink.

Sometimes she would even splurge on a donut or bagel, depending on how much money she had in her purse. She didn't really think about how she was spending her money because, as soon as she had a little bit of extra money, she would just use it however she wanted.

One day, her friends started a group chat and shared that one of their favorite indie bands was coming to their city. It had just been announced, and the concert was just a few weeks away. Wendy wanted to go more than anything, but she realized she didn't have any money to pay for the tickets. Ironically, as she was chatting with her friends in the group chat, she was also sipping on her strawberry lemonade. She decided she was going to ask her parents for more money so she could pay for the tickets. However, her parents said that since she gets an allowance, they weren't going to give her any more money. She was in charge of how she spent her allowance money, so if it was all used up, there was nothing they could do.

She slumped off to her room and fell face-first onto her bed. Out of the corner of her eye, she could see the strawberry lemonade sitting on her dressing table. She never thought she would regret her favorite drink, but she knew that if she didn't spend all of her money on Starbucks, she would have enough to go to the concert. On the day of the concert, all she could do was watch her friends' Instagram stories and lives. From that day on, she decided that she was going to start spending her money a little more wisely because she didn't want to end up in this position again.

WHAT IS A BUDGET?

Does this mean that Wendy will never get to have another Starbucks drink again? Absolutely not! The problem wasn't actually the Starbucks drink, but the fact that she wasn't budgeting her money properly. If she had been taught to budget, she would probably still have enough for one or two Starbucks drinks, plus the other things she wanted. Budgeting helps us create a plan for our money. A good budget allows us to still have fun but also save for the things that are more important to us. This way, we don't end up losing out in the end.

When you are able to create an effective budget, you get to be the one in control of your money. Your budget will be completely personal to you and your situation. This means that as you grow and your finances change, your budget will also change. Budgeting is actually a habit because you have to do it every week or every month. Doing this before you get paid is essential so you know where your money is going from the get-go. This helps you develop a healthy relationship with your money. It also allows you to save and plan for your future.

There are so many stories of adults who do not have a budget and end up in horrible financial situations. It is so easy to spend more money than you actually make and then get yourself into debt. Planning is the only way to avoid this, and that is why budgeting is so important. If you are able to learn this skill and implement it in your life, then you will already be ahead of your peers. Learning to budget at a young age means that you can do so in a safe environment. Right now, you probably don't have as many responsibilities as your parents or any other adult. This means you can learn to budget with a small amount of money and build the habit in a healthy way. When you are older and earning a larger salary, you won't struggle with budgeting and managing your money.

PICK A BUDGETING STRATEGY

Every person is different, and what works for one will probably not work for another. This also applies to budgeting. You have to find a budgeting strategy that will work for you. The good news is that there are many different budgeting strategies out there. You'll probably be able to find one that's perfect for you. You can also try a few budgeting strategies and then decide which one you think will work best for you. Handling finances is sometimes a trial-and-error thing, so don't feel bad if you have to switch up your strategy at some point.

The Pay Yourself First Strategy

The first strategy we are talking about is called pay yourself first. Typically, when we spend money, we are giving it to other people. For instance, helping to fund other people's salaries and helping your favorite business be profitable so they can continue to serve you (like Wendy buying her favorite drink from Starbucks). With budgeting, however, you will always be the most important person, and that is why you need to pay yourself before you pay anyone else.

Paying yourself means saving. It's saving for your future and for the things you really want down the line. You can actually implement this strategy into most other budgeting strategies. All it requires you to do is put money into your savings before you spend anywhere else. As soon as your allowance or salary comes into your pocket or bank account, you will take the amount you want to save and put it in a separate account. You can then use all the money that's left to spend however else you like. Saving is always the most important thing when it comes to budgeting and planning for your future. If you are new to handling finances, then this is a great place to start.

Zero-Based Budget

For someone who needs more structure in their budgeting approach, this is a great option. It allows you to track exactly where your money is going and make sure that you aren't wasting it on unnecessary things. Basically, you are allocating every dollar you earn to something in your budget. When you tally up your spending versus your income, you should get zero. This doesn't mean that you actually have to spend all the money you make. It just means that every dollar will have a purpose.

When you write out your budget, you will first take into consideration your income. Then you will put the money into the various categories in your budget. This will include things like savings, food, transportation, and entertainment. At the end of your budget, you should have no dollars left. You are basically deciding what you are spending your money on before you get a chance to spend it. This is a great method if you have a specific goal that you are trying to save toward and want to free up as much money as possible to save for it.

50/30/20 Strategy

This method highlights the percentages of your income that will go to various areas of your budget. Fifty percent will go to things that are essential to you. This will be like paying your bills, food, transportation, and other things that you absolutely have to pay for in the month. Thirty percent will go towards things that you want. These could be things like clothing, going out to eat, and a gym membership. These things might be important to you, but they are not a necessity for you to live. The final 20% will go towards your savings. You can implement the 'pay yourself first' strategy and take the 20% out of your income and deposit it straight into your savings account.

This type of strategy works amazingly well for most people because it provides balance. You aren't being too strict on your budget, but you are also making sure that money is going towards your savings and long-term goals. Everything has a place, but you don't have to sit and dictate exactly where each dollar goes. For those who are new to budgeting, this is a great way to get started.

CREATING A BUDGET PLAN

Regardless of the type of strategy you choose, you will still need to follow a few simple budgeting basics. This is where you create your budget plan and where you will decide where your money goes. Thankfully, it is a pretty simple process, and you can do it in a matter of minutes. Feel free to use whatever you want to create a budget. Some people prefer to go old-school with a simple piece of paper and a pen, while others love to use spreadsheets or even the Notes app on their phones.

Know Your Income

The first step in creating a budget is knowing what you are working with. This means you need to know how much money you make each month. If you have a part-time job, then you can add this to your income. Your allowance and any other money you get as gifts would also count. Your income could be the exact same each month, and this will make budgeting a lot easier. If you earn a different amount of money each month, then you should work from your average income. You can get an average from the previous three months and use that as your base. You will need to adjust each month when you get your salary or income. All you will need to do is add up all your different sources of income so you get the total, and then use that to budget.

Track Your Spending

Now that you know how much you are making, you need to make sure you do not spend more than you make. The best way to understand whether you are spending too much is to start tracking your spending. Most of us underestimate how much we spend in each category of our lives. We think we spend a lot less than we actually do, and this can lead us to create a budget that's not really accurate.

If you want to be accurate, you are going to have to start collecting some data. For the first month, try not to set any expectations for your spending. Just act and spend normally. Collect all your receipts or track them on your banking app. If you pay anything in cash, make sure to write it down or put it in your app. See where you are spending and how much you are spending in each category. This will give you a good idea of where your money is going and where you need to start cutting back. Here are some good apps to try: Mint, YNAB, and Goodbudget.

Decide on Your Goals

While you are busy tracking your spending and seeing where your money goes, you can also start deciding on your financial goals. These will be the things that are most important to you. Every person's financial goals will be different based on what is important to them. Some financial goals are for the long-term and others are short-term. You can have multiple financial goals running at the same time, but make sure you prioritize the most important ones. It can be difficult to save for multiple goals at a time, so if you know what's most important, you can take care of those first before moving on to the others.

The goals you set for yourself should be realistic. Make sure that you are incredibly specific with your goals and have set a timeframe within which you want to achieve them. This will make it a lot more likely that you will reach these goals. Many people set goals way too broadly, and it becomes difficult to make a plan to reach them. For example, you might say that one of your goals is to be financially independent. This sounds like a great goal, but what does it mean, and what is it going to take for you to get there? What does financially independent mean to you? Does that mean living in an apartment or a house, or maybe an RV? Find out how much it costs to live your lifestyle of financial independence and go for it. You may have to set several short-term goals to reach a long-term goal, like being financially independent. You can say your goal is to have X amount of money saved in X amount of time. This will help you create a plan to reach the goal. You know how much money you need and how long you have to save for it. Always try to make your goals as specific as possible so you have a greater chance of reaching them.

You can then split up each goal into monthly goals. So let's say you want to save $500 by the end of the year. This gives you 12 months to save $500. In order to reach this goal, you would need to save just over $40 per month. This goes into your budget, and once you have reached the goal, you can remove it from your budget and replace it with another goal. Remember to always be realistic with the goals that you set. They should be able to fit easily into your lifestyle based on your income. If you set goals that are way too big, it might be discouraging if you are unable to reach them.

Develop a Plan

Now that you have all of this information, it is time for you to start developing your plan and your budget. Use the information you gathered from tracking your spending to see where you spend your money the most.

You can start dividing your spending into different categories. Some categories you can consider are meals, gas money, phone bill, gym memberships, subscription services, clothes, entertainment, and grooming and beauty. You might have different categories based on your lifestyle, so make sure you look at where your money is going.

Now start to see how much you spend in each category. You will notice that certain categories have a lot more spending allocated to them than others. Take your categories and split them up based on your needs versus your wants. Your needs will probably be things like gas money and lunch money. These are things that you need every single month. Your wants would probably be the majority of the other things that we have just mentioned in the previous paragraph. If you noticed you were spending a lot of money in one category, you can mark this as a soft spot. This is a soft spot you have in your spending because you are more likely to blow your money in certain areas. Having this information means that you can look at your spending and see how you can avoid spending so much in categories that are not as important.

At this point, you would have discovered some of your financial goals and what you want to save for. This means saving is another priority you will be adding to your budget. If you have not been saving before this, it means that you're probably going to need to cut back on other areas of your budget. Have a look at things that are not as important to you or that you think you are spending on unnecessarily. You can start to cut down on your spending in those areas so you can take that money and put it into the areas that are more important.

Review and Adjust As Needed

Now that your budget is all ready to go, you will need to start using it. The first few months of budgeting are going to be a learning process. You will probably need to adjust your budget so that it suits your current spending and savings goals. If your goals change, then you would also need to adjust it based on that. Things like an increase in income or a birthday coming up where you get a lot of money as a gift can also impact your budget.

You might also realize that you are struggling to stick to your budget in certain areas. Ask yourself why this is. Is it because you have allocated too little money to that area or because you are spending too much? This will help you decide whether you need to adjust your budget or adjust your habits. If this is your first time following a budget, it can be a bit difficult. It means that you have to change the way you spend your money, so don't worry if you don't get it right immediately. Eventually, you will start to get used to it, and when you get closer and closer to your financial goals, it will all be worth it.

ACTIVITY: EXPERIMENT WITH THE DIFFERENT BUDGET MODELS

Below is a spreadsheet that you can use to create your own budget. It allows you to see how much money you make as well as how much money you are going to spend. It also prioritizes your savings. You can use the spreadsheet with any of the budgeting methods we spoke about in this chapter. If you are using the 'pay yourself first' method of budgeting, you will probably only need to fill out the income and saving portion of the budget. If you use the 50/30/20 method, you would need to allocate the correct amount based on the percentages in each step of the budget. If you are using the zero-based budgeting approach, you would need to make sure that your income matches the amount used from saving and spending combined.

Income

Source of Income	Estimated Amount	Actual Amount
Total		

Saving

Savings Type	Savings Goal	Actual Amount Saved
Total		

Spending

Spending Category	Amount Allocated	Amount Spent
Total		

ACTIVITY: MONEY SIMULATION - PLAN B

Whoops! It looks like you spent too much money last month, and now your budget is in the negative. This means that you have to rebalance your budget for this month. In order to do that, you would either need to make more money or save money in your budgeting categories. It might be even better if you can do both. The goal is to make sure that your budget goes back up to zero dollars or is a positive number.

For example, Max went over budget by $100. Instead of panicking, he looks at his budget and sees what he can do. The first thing he looks at is where he can cut back. He knows he is going roller skating for his friend's birthday next week. He was planning on renting skates, but that is going to cost $15. Instead, he remembers that his cousin has a pair and asks to borrow them. He also knows his neighbor often gets someone to mow his lawn, so he asks if he can do it for $50. The neighbor agrees, and now Jim has $65 to add to his budget. He could also chop wood for $25 and make his friend a gift instead of buying something, which will save him an additional $20. Now he has made up for overspending and is back on track.

Take some time to write out five ideas on how you can either save more money or make more money this month.

1. Idea: Amount made/saved:
2. Idea: Amount made/saved:
3. Idea: Amount made/saved:
4. Idea: Amount made/saved:
5. Idea: Amount made/saved:

ACTIVITY: TRACK YOUR SPENDING

Tracking your spending is going to take some work, but it is pretty straight forward. Use the below template to start tracking your spending in various categories. It is usually best to write down what you spend as you go. If you do not have this on hand, you can make a note of it in your notes app on your phone. Then, when you get home, you can fill this in.

Food:

Name	Amount Spent

Clothing:

Name	Amount Spent

Activities:

Name	Amount Spent

Subscriptions:

Name	Amount Spent

Grooming and Beauty:

Name	Amount Spent

Hobbies:

Name	Amount Spent

Other:

Name	Amount Spent

Creating a budget and knowing where your money is going is the first step to managing your finances. You actually won't be able to do anything else mentioned in this book effectively unless you have this down. Budgeting helps you enjoy your life now while saving for future goals. In the next chapter, we are going to be going through all things saving. Saving is a habit that is essential for your finances, but it is also one that many people (including adults) struggle with. However, if you know a few tips and tricks, you will be able to do it without a problem. In fact, it will become second nature!

2

MAKE SAVING MONEY A HABIT

Jonathan had a dream. A dream to go to a prestigious university, graduate with a degree that he was passionate about, start his dream job, and live a life where he was comfortable and happy. The problem was that his current home situation didn't look like it was going to support this type of dream. His home life wasn't that great. In fact, it was quite unstable, and he knew that his parents would never be able to afford to send him to a good university. Even though getting a student loan was always an option, it was not something that he wanted to do, or at least he wanted to take out as small a loan as he possibly could.

He spoke to his cousin, who had attended the university he wanted to attend. She took out a student loan, and even though she had finished university eight years ago, she was still paying it off. That was not something Jonathan wanted for himself. The only way he was going to get the money he needed for college was if he saved it himself. He had two years until he graduated from high school, so that meant two years of hard work. He was prepared for it, and even though he knew he wasn't going to be able to save up all the money he needed for college, he could save up quite a bit so his loan didn't have to be as large. He also planned to apply for a scholarship so he didn't have to take out a loan, but that was something he was going to think about a little later.

He got himself a part-time job and saved all his money towards his college tuition fees. He had a plan and knew how much he needed to save and how much he needed to make. If he saw he was falling a bit short, he would pick up a few extra hours so he could earn a bit more money. On his summer holidays, he would also choose to get jobs that were slightly higher-paying so he could focus on building up his savings. Even though this was a sacrifice for him, he was still able to enjoy his high school years while saving for his college tuition.

All his hard work paid off, and he was able to completely pay for his first year's tuition fees without taking out a loan. He continued working while he was studying for his degree so he could earn as much money as he could. He did have to take out a small loan, but it was not something major, and he quickly paid it off in the first two years of graduating college. Saving while he was still in high school allowed him to build up habits that he could take through his college years and working years. He was able to live his dreams and reach his goals by prioritizing his savings, and now he's living the lifestyle he really wants to.

STEPS TO SAVING

You might have the same savings goals as Jonathan, or maybe you have something completely different. It doesn't really matter what your savings goals are because the process is going to be very similar. As long as you have a realistic savings goal, you will be able to implement the steps in this section to help you save more.

Find Your Magic Number

The first thing you are going to need to do is find your number. This is the amount of money that you will be saving towards. The amount of money you will need will depend on what you're looking to buy or pay for. College tuition will definitely be a lot more expensive, while if you're looking to save for something like a new pair of sneakers, it's going to be cheaper.

Regardless of what you are trying to purchase, you should do some research to find out how much it's going to cost you. Once you fully understand this, you can lock in the number. You can also find out if your parents are willing to chip in for certain items, which will mean you have to save less money. Once you know how much you are responsible for saving, you can write it down and commit to it.

Set Some Aside

The next thing you will need to do is decide when you want to purchase the item. This will help you get a timeline so you know how much money you need to set aside every month. Saving is something you should be doing consistently, not just once in a while. If you break down a big savings goal into smaller sections, it will be a lot more manageable for you. If you want to buy a new pair of sneakers and you know they cost $150, you can set a timeline of three months to save for the shoes. This means that you would need to save $50 each month in order to reach your goal. This is very easy to track, and you can make sure you are saving the right amount of money every month.

Automatic Savings

If you are using a bank account to save your money, that's going to make things a lot easier. We will be talking more about bank accounts in the next chapter, but for now, just know that they are really helpful when it comes to finances. You can set up an automatic payment from your transactional account to your savings account, so you don't even have to think about saving. Every month, on a specific day, your bank deposits money into your savings account, and that's that. It makes saving a whole lot easier, and you don't have time to talk yourself out of it.

Make Some Changes to Your Spending

You might be able to save even more money if you look at what you are spending. It is very easy to overspend in certain areas, and this means you'll just have less money to save for things that are really important. Have a look at your spending and see where you can cut back. You won't have to cut back forever because as soon as you reach your savings goal, you can go back to spending your money as you usually would.

You can make a few spending trade-offs that still allow you to have what you want at a cheaper rate. For example, if you always buy lunch when you are at school, this can quickly add up. Instead, you can start packing lunch at home so you can use the money to save towards your most important goals.

Make More Money

It is always a good idea to keep track of how much you are saving and whether or not you're able to reach your end goal. If you notice that you are not saving as much as you want to, you can look into ways to make more money. There will always be a limited amount of money that you can save based on your current salary or allowance. Finding ways to make more money means that you will have more money to save.

If you have a part-time job, you can ask your employer if they are willing to add a few more hours so you can make more money. Perhaps you can ask your parents to increase your allowance if you do more chores around the house. You could also look into taking up a side hustle or looking for another way to make some extra cash. You definitely don't want to burn yourself out by working too much, so make sure you know how much capacity you have and then work from there.

SPENDING WANTS VS. NEEDS

When you are thinking about spending, you need to identify the things that you want versus the things that you need. This is going to really help you when you try to save and cut back on your spending. The things that you need will be very difficult to cut back on because these are your necessities. They include things like your housing, transportation, food, and utilities.

Then your wants are the things that are not as important but do add something to your life. You can go without them if you absolutely need to. These can include entertainment, clothing, eating out, and travel. The things you want basically help you to live a more comfortable life. It's things that you enjoy having or enjoy doing. This can be different based on the person, so you need to look at your own life and determine the things that you truly want.

It is important to differentiate between the two, but sometimes it can be difficult. It is easy to think we need something when we really don't. As a teenager, you might not have many needs that you have to pay for yourself. This means that most of your spending will be in the wants category, and you can probably cut back on those things. If you are not sure, make a list of all of your expenses and divide them into the two categories.

Be completely honest with yourself and decide whether or not you need certain things in order to live or whether they're just helping you live a more comfortable life.

Before you start thinking you can't have any nice things in your life or that your wants are not important, you can definitely enjoy your money. Your wants are important because these are the things that help you enjoy life. However, they are just not at the top of the priority list. You will only need to cut back on these things when you are saving up for something that requires a bit more sacrifice.

BECOME A SMART SPENDER

Learning how to spend smarter can help you to save better. You will be able to save some money from your spending to put away in your savings account. This is a habit that you have to build because it doesn't come naturally. It takes some time to learn how to be a smart spender, but once you do, you will quickly see the benefits.

Compare Prices

When you are looking for a certain item there will probably be quite a few shops that sell it. Many people just buy the first thing they see, but this can lead to spending way more than necessary. The best way to avoid this is to compare prices before you shop. This way, you know where you can get the cheapest option, and you won't be overspending.

Since we all have the internet at our disposal, we can use it to check out the prices of items at different stores. If you want to shop at a mall and there are no online sources to find out the prices, you can do a price-check shopping trip and then a purchasing shopping trip. This will still allow you to check out the prices and then decide where the best place to buy will be. Make sure to take notes on the cheapest prices and where to get them.

Find Alternatives and Substitutes

There are so many alternatives to spending so you really don't have to spend all your money to have some fun. If there is something you want to do or buy, look for a cheaper way to do it. If you and your friends want to go to the movies on a Friday evening, why not substitute that for a movie-night sleepover? You can also ask everyone to bring their favorite snacks so you have tons of options. If you want to redecorate your room, instead of buying all new items, try DIY projects that you can do for much less. You might even find some interesting stuff in the attic or garage that you can use for your room. There are tons of ways you can spend less money if you look for alternatives. It just takes some time and a little creativity.

Keep a Record of Your Purchases

One of the best ways to stop spending so much is to write down each of your purchases. This is like a subconscious way to keep you on track. It adds an extra layer of commitment to the purchase. It might seem like such a small thing, but it makes a huge difference. You will notice that you end up thinking more about your purchases because you are less impulsive. I would suggest writing it down before making the purchase. This way, you create some buffer time to think about whether or not you actually want to buy the thing.

Discount Codes Are Your Friends

Many companies offer discount codes when you buy certain items. This can cut down the amount you pay by quite a bit. Now, this is only going to save you money if you only buy things you really need. After you have decided you need or want something, you can take some time to search for discount codes. You might even want to look at influencers and YouTubers' pages to see if they have been advertising the products you want to buy. Just look in the YouTube description box or caption, and you should find it and be able to apply it at checkout.

ACTIVITY: SHORT-TERM FINANCIAL GOALS

It is important for you to figure out a few financial goals for yourself. If you have never set a financial goal, then starting with a short-term goal is usually best. This way, you can see your goals come to life rather than waiting a really long time to reach them. Many people end up getting discouraged if their goals take too long to reach. As you start setting more goals and realize that you are able to reach them, you can start setting longer-term goals.

A short-term goal is one that you can reach in a few weeks up to about two months. Some people say a short-term goal is up to three months, but let's stick to two while you are first starting out with goal setting. Your goal could be to save up for something, or it could not involve money at all. Here are some examples of short-term financial goals:

- Save $100 in your savings account.
- Buy a mother's or father's day gift.
- Save up to donate to your favorite charity.

- Guitar lessons in the summer.
- Spending money for an upcoming vacation.
- A new item of clothing.
- A new video game.
- Shoes for prom.
- Open a savings account.
- Research scholarships for college for one hour a week.
- Apply for your very first job.

These are just ideas, but your goals could be anything mentioned or something completely different. Try to choose one short-term goal and do your best to reach it. Once that is done, you can try another. This will help you build the habit.

ACTIVITY: 30-DAY SAVINGS CHALLENGE

I'm not going to lie to you. Saving can sometimes be hard. If you are a competitive person, then setting a challenge for yourself can be really helpful. It will motivate you to keep going so you can feel that sense of accomplishment when you get to the finish line. We are using a dollar in this example, but you could use dimes or quarters to accomplish the same activity. This is just a 30-day challenge, so it isn't even that long.

Day 1 to 5: Save $1 each day

Day 5 to 10: Save $2 each day

Day 11 to 15: Save $3 each day

Day 16 to 20: Save $4 each day

Day 21 to 30: Save $5 each day

By the end of the month, you will have $100 saved up. You can use this for whatever you want. This trains you to save because you are doing it every day.

When I was younger, we had to save all our money somewhere safe. I chose to save it under my mattress, while some of my friends had piggy banks. I had another friend who used a sock in his drawer as his secret money stash. These days, it is way better to open up a bank account to put your money into. When you are older, you will need to have a bank account if you don't have one already. This is where your salary will be deposited, and it is a safe place to keep all your money. If banking confuses you, don't worry, you are not alone. In the next chapter, we are going to be talking about all things banking.

3

BANKING FOR YOUR NEEDS

B anking is not something that only adults can do. Back in the day, it might have been a little bit harder for teenagers to open up a bank account, but these days it's pretty easy. You will need your parents' help with this, but the process doesn't take that long. This means that you can also have a very safe way to store your money and get all the other benefits that come with banking.

WHAT ARE THE DIFFERENT ACCOUNTS?

There are tons of different banking accounts that you could have. Banks will have different options for different people and their needs. It's important to understand all your banking options so you can make the right choice for you. Remember that every banking account will have different benefits as well as different fees that you will need to pay. Doing your research on the various types of bank accounts your bank offers will help you make the right choice. You can also shop around at different banks, so you can compare prices that way. Ask your parents for some help with this. They might be with a certain bank and really love it for a particular reason.

Savings Account

A savings account is exactly what it sounds like. This is an account where you will deposit all your savings. The benefit of this type of account is that it has a higher interest rate. This is because you are leaving your money there for a longer period of time.

You will be able to make regular payments into your savings account so that it is safe. The longer you keep your savings in your savings account, the more interest you will gain. This is also a great place to keep your money if you are saving for a specific thing. You will still have access to all of your money, so as soon as you have enough, you can take out the money from your account and purchase what you want. Some savings accounts are locked in for a specific time, and the interest rate will be higher. If you have a specific long-term goal, then this type of savings account is a great way to remove the temptation to withdraw money from the account.

Checking Accounts

A checking account can be looked at as a transactional account. This is where you will keep money and be able to swipe your card to make purchases or withdraw from an ATM to take out funds. These accounts are very easy to access so you can purchase whatever you want with the money available in your account. You can use a debit card, ATM, or check to spend your money. It is a great way to keep your money safe so you don't have to carry around cash all the time. If you have a job or a part-time job, your salary can be deposited directly into your checking account.

Make sure you know how much money is in your checking account, because you will not be able to spend more than that. Once the money runs out in the account, you will not be able to use your debit card or withdraw from an ATM. If you write a check and the person goes to cash it, the check will bounce back and you might incur fees. This is why it is important to budget for the money you have in your checking account. You can keep all the receipts from your trans-actions so you are aware of how much money you have left in your account. If you use online banking, then you'll have access to an app where you can quickly check how much money is in your account.

Money Market Accounts

A money market account is like a hybrid of a checking account and a savings account. The interest that you earn on this type of account is typically much higher, but you can also write checks and withdraw money from it. However, most teenagers will not be able to open this account because there is usually a minimum balance requirement. This means that you have to have a certain amount of money in order to open this account. This amount can be well into the thousands, and that's why most teenagers don't choose this option. When you are older and have more money to deposit into the account, you can think about it as a great option to earn interest and have your money easily accessible to you.

Investment Accounts

Investment accounts are a bit different from the other accounts we have mentioned. Instead of putting your money in the account in order to spend it later, you are investing it so you can earn more money. This is usually done by earning interest or even dividends from the investments in the account. Many times, you will have an advisor or a fund manager who will help you decide where to invest your money. Then you can expect returns on your investment by a certain date. This is usually a longer-term commitment because you do have to invest for a good amount of time to see an increase in your money that is worth something. You can use an investment account to save for something like retirement or another long-term financial goal.

OPENING A BANK ACCOUNT (WITH PARENTS)

Now that you know the different types of bank accounts, you are probably ready to open one for yourself. You will need one of your parents to go with you to help open your bank account if you are under the age of 18.

How to Open a Bank Account

Before you decide to open a bank account, you should do your research on the different banks and what they offer. Remember to take into account the fees that you will be paying because you don't want to pay too much for a simple bank account. There are some bank accounts that might be free or really cheap for students and teenagers. If you have a job that auto-deposits your salary, many banks will offer you free checking for depositing your paycheck into your account with their bank.

When you get to the bank to open your account, you will need a few documents. You can go online to check out what documents your specific bank needs to open an account. Typically, you will need to bring a verified form of ID, such as your government photo ID, driver's license, or passport. You would also need to bring proof of address. Check if there is a minimum deposit needed to open the bank account because you will need to bring this money with you so you can deposit it into the account. Since this is a student or teenage banking account, it is likely that the amount is not going to be too high. Your parent will also need to bring along identification for themselves to prove that they are your parent. If you are confused about what you need, you can also call the bank and speak to a consultant.

When you arrive at your appointment, the consultant will guide you through the process. This might include taking your biometrics and a photo. You will also be notified of the benefits and costs of the bank account. There will also be a few documents you will need to sign to acknowledge that you are opening a bank account and can sustain it. Make sure you read the paperwork so you are aware of what is required of you. You should get a copy of this to take home so you always have something to reference. After all of this is done, your bank account should be ready to go, and then you will receive your card and be able to swipe away.

Some banks have an online application service that you can use. This is definitely an easier option, and you know you will have all the documents on hand at your house. The application online shouldn't take more than a few minutes, and it's pretty self-explanatory. You'll be guided through what needs to be uploaded and the questions that need to be answered. Remember to do this with your parents so you can ensure it is done correctly. After the online application is submitted, you will have to wait a few days until it is approved and your card is sent to you.

Features to Look Out For

Every bank and bank account is different and has different features. The features that you need will be based on your lifestyle and what you're looking for in a bank and bank account. Some helpful features will include a debit card, app alerts or messages when trans-actions take place, limits to spending and withdrawals, and the ability to transfer money between accounts.

The Benefits

There are tons of benefits to opening a bank account when you are younger. Firstly, you will be able to manage and handle your money in a safe place. When you get older, you will need a bank account to keep all of your money in, so if you are aware of how banks and bank accounts work, you will be in a better position. They also help you keep track of your money because you can get statements showing where and when you swipe your card and spend your money.

You'll be able to develop some money habits quite early on in your life. This can help you have a healthy relationship with finances from a young age. Since your parents or guardians will be watching over you and your bank account, they will also be able to guide you. This means that you can learn in a safe way and have guidance from those who are older than you.

THE MAGIC OF COMPOUND INTEREST

Have you ever seen a magic show as a kid? There is always one trick that the magician or clown does all the time. It's the one where they have a handkerchief in their pocket or in their sleeve, and they ask someone to pull on it. Once the volunteer starts pulling, more and more handkerchiefs keep coming out. It seems like a never-ending stream of handkerchiefs, and it usually has all the kids mesmerized. What looks like something small turns out to grow into something really big the longer the person pulls.

This is a really fun magic trick. When it comes to money, we have something similar called interest. While you're not going to be pulling money out of your sleeve, it's all about growing your money over time. The longer you leave your money in an account that grows with interest, the bigger the amount will get. So you might deposit one handkerchief (a few dollars), but you will get hundreds in return. This is truly the magical effect of interest, and it's such an important concept to learn while you're still young.

There are two main forms of interest, compound interest and simple interest. You probably have some sort of basic understanding of what simple interest is. Simple interest is the interest that you earn on the amount you have deposited in the bank. Let's say you deposit $1,000 into a bank account that earns five percent simple interest per year. At the end of the year, you would earn $50 worth of interest. This means that your investment will now be $1,050. Because simple interest works based on the amount you invest, you will continue to gain $50 every single year.

For compound interest, you can have the same thousand dollars and the same interest rate with the only difference being that it is now compounded. So you have $1,000 at a five percent compound interest rate each year. Compound interest not only takes into account the amount invested but also the interest earned. This means you'll be earning interest on top of your interest. After the first year, you will have $1,051.16. This doesn't look like a huge difference from the simple interest earned in the previous example. However, let's look at what would happen to your investment after two years. You would have $1,104.94. With simple interest, you would just have $1,100. You can see the compound interest investment is slowly increasing.

Let's look ahead and see what your compound interest investment would look like over time. In five years, you would have $1,283.36; in 10 years, you would have $1,647.01; in 20 years, you would have $2,712.64; in 30 years would be $4,467.74; And 40 years would be a huge jump to $7,358.42. Now you can see your money is basically doubling every 10 years. After 40 years with simple interest, you would have around $3,000 in your investment account. This is why choosing an account that gives you compound interest is so important. Your money ends up doubling over time and you don't have to do much.

The examples given are very basic examples so you can see how compound interest works. However, when you are investing, you will be putting money away every single month. This means that even if you start off with $1,000 in your investment account every month, you will be increasing the amount. This will mean your investment grows a whole lot faster, and you will be able to reach large amounts saved in your compound interest investment account. This is one of the best hacks when it comes to growing your money. Compound interest allows you to make money without having to do anything. When you are looking for an investment account, make sure you are earning compound interest instead of simple interest.

ACTIVITY: CALCULATE COMPOUND INTEREST

Take some time to play around with compound interest. You can add different figures to an online calculator to see how your money will grow over time. You can use this calculator: Compound Interest Calculator. Alternatively, you can just type 'compound interest calculator' into your search bar and you will have a few options to choose from.

ACTIVITY: BANKING BASICS QUIZ

Question 1: What is the name of the bank account where you can deposit your money and earn interest on it?

Question 2: What documents might you need to open your bank account?

Question 3: What is the type of interest where you earn interest on top of interest?

Question 4: What is the type of bank account from which your salary will be paid, and you can make transactions?

Question 5: Name two benefits to look out for when opening your first bank account.

- **Answer 1:** Savings account.
- **Answer 2:** Some type of photo ID, proof of residence, and parents' documents.
- **Answer 3:** Compound interest.
- **Answer 4:** Checking account.
- **Answer 5:** Choose any two: banking alerts, debit cards, withdrawal limits, spending limits, or the ability to transfer money to different accounts.

4

CREDIT AND YOU

The average American has $6,194 in credit card debt (White, 2020). If you aren't careful, credit cards can get out of hand. There are so many people who take out credit cards with good intentions, and then it just spirals out of control. It can be really tempting to spend on a credit card because the money is just there to use. A credit card can be a very useful tool when you know how to use it properly.

CREDIT CARDS

In many coming-of-age movies, there is always a scene where the main character goes on a huge shopping spree. This is usually because there's a special event coming up or they are redefining the way they look.

The quintessential movie shot is when the character starts swiping their credit cards. It seems so easy, and the character looks like they are having the time of their life. With this mental picture, it is easy to see how people tend to overspend when it comes to credit cards. A simple swipe and you just get whatever you want. Who doesn't want that?

Credit cards can definitely be used to buy things you want, but they can also get you into a whole lot of debt. When you use a credit card just to buy things for the sake of it, you can end up creating some negative money habits that will carry consequences for a long time in the future. You see, the money on a credit card is technically not your money. This is money that you are borrowing and you will need to pay back with interest. Credit cards have a higher interest rate than many other types of loans or debt.

Let's take a moment to explain credit cards a little bit more. When you sign up for a credit card, the bank will look at your credit records and decide how much they are willing to lend you. This is not a once-off type of loan. It is known as a revolving credit. Every month, you will have a specific amount that you are allowed to spend on your credit card. You won't be able to go over this amount, but you also don't have to pay it back immediately if you do spend it. You will have to pay back a percentage of what you owe each month. This percentage amount is decided on by the bank and is usually a small percentage of the total amount that you owe. This means you can spend a large amount today, but only need to pay it back in the months or years to come.

This sounds like an awesome plan if you really want something but don't have the money right now. The problem is that it can be very difficult to pay off a credit card if you only pay the minimum. The minimum amount will usually only take care of the interest earned, so you will still need to pay back the amount you actually borrowed. The longer you don't pay off your credit card, the more money you will be paying back. Let's say you owe $1,000 on a credit card with 12% interest per year or one percent per month. The bank says that you need to pay back a five percent minimum on your balance. This will allow your credit card to still be in good standing, and you can continue borrowing if you need to. It is a requirement to pay the minimum each month. Have a look at this table:

Month	One Percent Interest Owed	Five Percent Required Payment	New Balance Owed
1	$10	$50.5	$959.5
2	$9.60	$48.45	$920.65
3	$9.20	$46.50	$883.35
4	$8.83	$44.61	$847.57

As you can see, it is going to take a very long time to pay off this credit card, and this is assuming the person never uses it for anything else. This is why it is so important to make sure you fully understand credit cards and how they work. The minimum payment required helps the bank because you will continuously need to pay them. However, this does not help you.

If you cannot pay the minimum amount in any given month, then you will get hit with late fees. This means you will end up owing even more than what you currently owe. On top of that, it can impact your credit score in a negative way. If you use a credit card, it's always important to have a plan for how you're going to pay it back and make sure that you do not just pay back the minimum.

Not everyone needs credit cards, but there are definite benefits to having them. For one, if you have a credit card, you can use it in a case of an emergency or unforeseen circumstance. This will help you handle the emergency quickly and then pay back the money a bit later. Credit cards also have benefits and rewards tied to them. You can get cash back for things like study materials, gas, or even rent. The type of rewards you get from your credit card will depend on the account you open and the bank that issued it to you. One of the biggest benefits of a credit card is that it helps you build your credit score. Having a good credit score is essential when you want to make a big purchase like a house. It shows that you are trustworthy and will be able to pay back the loan. You just have to make sure that you're handling your credit card wisely.

Can You Get a Credit Card as a Teenager?

In most cases, you'll only be able to get a credit card when you are over the age of 18, and sometimes over the age of 21. There are different rules for different states and areas, so make sure that you are fully aware of what you are allowed to do in your area. It can definitely be beneficial to get a credit card as early as possible. This is because you can start building up credit as soon as you reach adulthood, so you can start making important purchases. With that being said, getting a credit card at a young age is not necessary. If you are not used to managing your money and handling your finances, then it is usually better to skip out on getting a credit card for now.

If you are unable to manage your money, then it is more likely that you will mess up with your credit card. Handling a credit card is a skill, and you need some practice so you can do it right. I would suggest focusing on budgeting and handling your money well first. Once you feel confident and are able to set financial goals that you can aim for and stick to, then you can look into getting a credit card.

There are ways for teenagers to get a credit card and start building up their credit score. One way is to become an authorized user on a parent's credit card. Your parents would already need to have a credit card and could then add you as an authorized user. You will get a separate card that is attached to their credit account. Any purchases you make or debt you incur will reflect on their credit score. Your parents may need some convincing to agree to this, and they might have some rules and conditions for you. Even if you never use the card yourself, their good credit history will also be reflected in your credit score, provided the account is in good standing and has a good payment history.

If you are over the age of 18 and cannot get approved for a credit card, there are ways you can still build up your credit score. One way is to cosign a credit card with someone else. It would be best if this person is one of your parents or a close family member. The person who co-signs with you will need to have a good credit history. If you are unable to pay back your credit card, they will be responsible for it. This means their credit score will also be impacted if you are not able to manage your finances properly. Another way to get credit at a young age is to open a secured credit card.

This works exactly like a normal credit card, but you will need to make an upfront deposit in order for your credit limit to be set. It gives some security to the bank so they are willing to offer credit to younger people.

With all of the ways that you can get a credit card at a younger age, there are also plenty of scams out there. If the financial institution that is offering you a credit card does not sound legit or the offer sounds too good to be true, then run in the other direction. These scams can hurt you and completely plummet your credit score. Often, the interest rates are incredibly high, making it very difficult to pay them back. The scammers might also just try to get your information so they can use it for nefarious purposes. This is why it is important to do your research and ensure that you only use reputable financial service providers.

CREDIT SCORES

Your credit score is just a number or figure that shows people how likely you are to pay back any money that you have borrowed. There are tons of factors that impact your credit score. It is important to focus on all of these factors to make sure that you have a good credit score. There are a few different credit bureaus that create a credit score. This means that there are different types of credit scores that you could access.

The two most common are the FICO score and the VantageScore. They are calculated slightly differently because each company will have its own algorithms to work out how likely you are to pay back your loans and credit.

The FICO score is the most popular credit rating system that is used by lenders. The score ranges anywhere between 300 and 850. The average score that is considered good is between 670 and 739. This will probably get you the majority of the loans you would wish to have, but there is still work to be done. The goal should be to have a very good or exceptional score because then you will receive the best rates from any lender. Remember that your credit score not only increases the likelihood of you getting a loan but also reduces the interest rates and fees you will pay in order to get the loan. Lenders will increase their rates if there is a risk involved in lending your money. Aiming to get over 740 is a very good score, and an exceptional score is over 800. Keep in mind, however, that you will have to wait about six months after you open your credit card before you get your score.

The VantageScore uses the same range as the FICO score, so you're still looking at a number between 300 and 850. Anything below 600 is a poor score on the scale. A good credit score would be 661 to 780. An excellent one would be above 781. With the VantageScore, your score is calculated as soon as you open up your very first credit account.

Each of these different types of credit scores is worked out slightly differently, but they do take into account the same type of information. If you want your FICO score, it will be calculated based on five different criteria. Each one of these five aspects will account for more or less of the overall credit score. Payment history and amounts owed are the two criteria that hold the most weight at 35% and 30%, respectively. Fifteen percent goes to how long you've had a credit history. Credit mix and new credit take 10% each.

With the VantageScore, there are six different criteria needed. The one that holds the most weight is payment history, which accounts for 40% of the score. Twenty-one percent goes to the length of credit, and 20% goes to credit utilization. Your current balances will be 11%, and any recent credit taken out will account for five percent. The final three percent will be your available credit.

You will always have access to your credit report for free, so you can easily look it up. If you have not taken out any credit, then you will not have a credit score. You should always take a look at your credit score before you take out any new loans or get a new credit card. This way, you can prepare for whether or not you will get one at a good rate. If your credit score is on the lower end, you can take some time to build it up before taking out a new credit card or a new loan. You can go directly through credit bureaus to check your credit score, and all of this can be done online. Your bank or credit union will also have this option so you can use the tools available there.

Using a Credit Card to Build a Healthy Credit Score

Once you take out your credit card, you can use it to build up your credit score. A credit card can either work to your advantage or to your detriment. Being able to use it well from the time you take it out is essential to having a healthy relationship with money and making sure that your credit score is always as high as it possibly can be.

As soon as you have been approved for your credit card and it has been delivered to you, you can start using it. However, you need a foolproof plan for how you are going to use your credit card so that you don't get carried away. Credit cards can impact your credit score very easily. Even if you miss just one payment, this can cause your score to drop over 100 points. This is why it is essential to pay your credit card off on time. You need to make sure you always have enough for at least the minimum payment on your credit card. Then you need to know when your credit card bill is due so you can handle it before then.

When I was describing how your credit score is calculated, I mentioned credit utilization. This may sound very fancy, but it is actually just how often and how much you are using or spending on your credit card. It is a good idea to keep your credit utilization on the lower end of the spectrum. If you keep maxing out your credit cards, this will impact your score negatively. You should try to limit your spending to a 30% utilization rate, but if you are trying to improve your credit score, a 10% utilization rate or lower is best. This means that if you have a credit card with a limit of $1,000 you should only be spending $100 since this is 10% off your total credit.

One of the best strategies to build credit without overdoing it is to work it into your budget. Pick something in your budget that is around the same amount each month. This could be groceries, gas money, or lunch money. Since these things typically equal the same amount each month, you can be sure that you will not overspend in these areas. You can swipe your credit card when you are purchasing these items, but make sure that you have that money in your debit card or your savings account. At the end of the month, you can put the money back into your credit card so you are not charged interest. This way, you are still using your credit card, but there is no risk of you overspending and ending up in a large amount of debt.

ACTIVITY: CREDIT SCORES

In this activity, you are going to be a credit counselor. This means that you get to advise someone on what they should do to improve their credit scores. Your client's name is Melissa Spendly. Below is her profile, which outlines exactly what she has done with her credit in the past few years. Place a + next to the statements you think will increase her credit score and a - next to the statements you think will lower your credit score.

- She opened her first credit card three years ago.
- She has two credit cards as of now, and both are in good standing.
- She missed a payment four months ago because it slipped her mind when she went on vacation.
- She took out a student loan two years ago.
- As of now, she has $10,000 outstanding on the student loan.
- She has not missed a student loan payment.

- She has never declared bankruptcy or gone through any other kind of negative proceeding.

- With this information, do you think you can work out her credit score? If you had to guess, what would her credit score be?
- Do you think she is likely to get a loan or line of credit at a good rate?
- What would you recommend Melissa do in order to improve her credit score?

ACTIVITY: SHOPPING WITH INTEREST

In this activity, you will be planning how to spend your money with a credit card. This is designed to show you how much more you will be spending when you shop with a credit card due to the interest. If you ever find yourself in a position where you do have to pay with a credit card, it is a good idea to plan and understand how much you really will be paying.

For this example, you have a credit card with an interest rate of 15%. If you use the credit card and there is a balance owed on it, the minimum payment you would need to make each month is four percent of the starting balance. With this information, you are able to plan the interest you will owe as well as how much you will actually be paying for the item.

Do some research on a few things that you might want to spend some money on. Check out the real prices and use this information to fill out the table below. The first row is already filled out as an example. You can use this Credit Card Calculator to help you, or you can type it into your search bar and find one to use for yourself.

Item Description	Price	Minimum Monthly Payment	Interest Owed	Time Taken to Pay it Off (only minimum paid)	Total Cost of the Item
New video game	$80	$3.20	$16	31 months	$96

5

AVOIDING THE DEBT TRAP

Did you know that 74% of people who fall under Gen Z and took out a student loan end up delaying big financial decisions because of the weight of this financial burden (Porter, 2021)? That's a crazy amount of people who cannot make smart financial decisions because they are tied down by large amounts of debt. Debt can be so difficult to escape, but it's important that you understand what this is and how to get out of it if you find yourself there. It is even more important to completely avoid bad debt if you can.

LOANS & BORROWING

Whenever you take out a loan or even a line of credit, you are essentially borrowing money from someone else. There are two people in the deal: the borrower and lender. The borrower needs some extra money to buy something they really need or want. The lender has the money and would be willing to give it to the borrower at a cost. The lender is essentially providing a service and will need to be compensated fairly for the service. As a lender, there's always a risk that the borrower will not pay you back. This is why credit scores exist, so lenders can keep their money safe. They don't want to lose out in the end. The riskier it is to lend money to someone, the higher the interest rate will be so it can offset the risk.

When you take out a loan, you are essentially borrowing money from a bank or another financial service provider. You will then work out a deal that, hopefully, works for both of you. In the contract, it will stipulate how much money you are borrowing, how much interest you'll need to pay back, and how long you will be borrowing the money for. Once the contract is signed, the lender will give you the money agreed upon, and you can use it however you like. After this, you would need to follow the payment plan setup so you can pay off the loan. You will have to pay at least the minimum every single month, but you are also free to pay more than the minimum so you can pay off the loan faster. Loans that offer balloon payments (where you pay a small amount back each month, leaving a large amount due at the end of the loan term) and pre-pay penalty clauses (where you get charged a fee if you want to pay the loan off early) are red flags and should be avoided. Loans are different from credit because, with a loan, you get one lump sum of money.

There are many reasons people might need a loan in order to purchase something. Big purchases like a car, college tuition, a house, or starting your own business are some good reasons. Sometimes people still take out loans even if they have the cash available. The reason they do this is so that they can keep their money, just in case. Even if you have $100,000 in the bank, it might not be the best move to use all of that money to pay for a big purchase. It might be safer to take out a loan and pay it off quickly so you still have access to your cash if you need it for an emergency or another purchase. A person might also want to take out a loan because all of their cash is tied up in other investments or other areas of their finances. If you are looking to take out a loan at some point in your life, it is always a good idea to do all your research and make sure you understand all of your options.

As a teenager, it can be difficult to fully understand how taking out a loan could impact your finances. In most cases, you will not be able to take out a loan by yourself at this age. However, you can simulate taking out a loan so you can understand the process and how it works. In order to do this, you will have to rope in a parent, family member, or maybe a teacher. Let them know that you want to simulate taking out a loan from them. Perhaps you have something that you want to buy, but you don't have the money right now. Let's say it's a new pair of sneakers. The sneakers cost $150, and you only have $50 to pay for them. You would need to borrow $100 from your parents or a guardian.

In order to make this realistic, take some time to draw up some paperwork so you both can see exactly what your roles are in this loan. You will need to understand the total amount that you are borrowing, the interest rate the lender will be imposing on you, the payment schedule, the due date for the monthly payment, and the total payment. You can even set up a penalty if you do not pay to make it interesting and even more realistic.

Since you are just borrowing $100, it's probably not going to take you that long to pay off the loan. Make sure that your repayment strategy is something that you can sustainably do over the next few months. Remember that you're not just paying back the hundred dollars but are also paying back the interest that is latched on to the amount. The longer you take to pay back the loan, the more money you will end up paying. Doing this short exercise will help you fully understand how borrowing and lending work and whether or not it is the best option in certain circumstances. It will also help you to think things through when you do reach a point in your life when taking out a loan is something you are truly considering.

GOOD DEBT VS. BAD DEBT

Whenever we talk about debt, everyone seems to only talk about the bad side. Most of what we have discussed in this book is the negative side of taking on debt. This is because most people tend to use it the wrong way. What happens is, they purchase things that they don't really need, and then their debt becomes too difficult for them to handle. However, there is definitely a way to use or leverage debt in a way that can help you manage your finances and reach your goals.

The Good

Let's first talk about good debt. Good debt allows you to leverage your money so you are able to purchase items that could increase your net worth in the future. For example, taking out a mortgage is a form of good debt because you are buying something that will increase in value over time. Another form of good debt could be investing in your education. If you must take out a student loan in order to pay for your degree, this could pay off in the future. You'll put yourself in a position where you can earn more money with a good job. This will then allow you to quickly pay off the debt so you have benefited from it. Another really good example of good debt is when you take out a business loan. If you are looking to start your own business but do not have the capital to get it going, then taking out a loan is a good option. The goal is to build up your business to a point where it is really successful and you are making a large amount of profit. This way, the debt becomes worth it.

With all of this being said, it is really important to know that a form of good debt can turn into a bad investment and therefore bad debt. Whenever you are planning on taking out any kind of loan or line of credit, you need to be sure that it is going to pay off in the end. There is always going to be some sort of risk involved when you take out a loan, but you need to make sure that you've done your research so the risk is not as high. For example, if you are looking to take out a student loan so you can go to college, you need to make sure the degree you will study has future job prospects. There are some degrees that lead to careers that pay more, and other degrees where it's very difficult to get a job in that field of study. Taking out a student loan for a degree in a career path that is not stable might not be the best option. However, taking out a student loan to pursue a career in something that has multiple job prospects and is high-earning is a great option. This is why doing your research is essential whenever you are planning on putting yourself into debt.

The same goes for starting a business. You need to make sure that your business idea is something that is marketable and buildable. Doing research on the current market surrounding the product or service you want to provide is essential. For example, you might want to start a dog-walking business. You notice that there aren't any dog-walking businesses in your area, so you think this is going to be a great idea. However, you need to ask yourself why there isn't already an established dog-walking business in your town or city. After doing some research, you realize that most people don't own dogs and actually prefer cats in your area. The reason there isn't a dog walking business in your area is because there aren't many people who need dog walkers in the first place. While this might have been a great business idea, it is not going to work in your city, so taking out a loan would be a form of bad debt because the business has a high likelihood of failing.

Since taking out any kind of debt is a large financial commitment, you always need to ensure that you are aware of the risks and possible benefits. I don't want you to be scared of taking out a loan for something that is important to you, and that could increase your financial standing in the future. However, it is always a good idea to take some time to pause and think through your decisions so you can be sure you're making the right ones.

The Bad

Bad debt is the type of debt that you are probably more familiar with. This is when you take out a loan or line of credit to buy things that are not necessary. Most people who land in debt do so because they try to live outside of their means. Living outside your means is when you live a certain lifestyle that is more expensive than what you can afford. In most cases, if you can't pay for the item directly, you probably don't need it or should look for alternatives.

There are plenty of forms of bad debt, but one that people don't often talk about is our cars. For some reason, the marketing around buying a vehicle makes it seem like a really good investment. Let me tell you something: just because an item is expensive doesn't mean it's a good investment. A car is actually a money guzzler and does not provide you with any financial benefit. I'm not trying to say that buying a car is not important. If you need transportation to get around, then you will probably need to buy a car, but you should never think of it as a good investment. If you buy a brand new car, as soon as you leave the car lot, it decreases in value. This means that you will never be able to sell your car for more than what you paid for it. It will always go down in price. Not only that, but you have to take into consideration all the money you will be pouring into your car for maintenance and gas.

Taking out a large loan to buy a brand new car might not be the best option. You can probably get a very good car at a fraction of the price if you buy second-hand. There are tons of secondhand cars that are in wonderful condition, and you can get great deals on them. As long as you do your research and have the car checked out, you should be good to go. That way, you don't have to get yourself into a large amount of debt for something that doesn't have any financial benefit to you. Buying a secondhand car is actually a great idea when it is your first one. Your first vehicle isn't meant to be fancy or the most expensive thing ever. Since you are just learning how to drive and navigate the roads, it is usually best to get a vehicle you don't mind getting a few scratches on. Then, when you are older, you can look into getting the new Mercedes you have been googling in between classes!

Store credit is also a very common type of debt that people take out. You probably have a few favorite clothing stores that offer store credit. When you have this card, you are able to purchase clothing and other items and only pay for them later. This is like a credit card, but only for a particular store. The truth is, you probably don't need the clothing or the items that are on offer. These are more of a luxury, and getting into debt for things that are not a necessity is definitely not smart. Credit cards and store credit can all be forms of bad debt because you end up spending more than is necessary. It is very easy to overspend in these areas and then end up in a bad financial position.

Another form of bad debt that you might not be familiar with is called a payday loan. These are some of the worst loans to ever take out because the interest rates are ridiculous. With these types of loans, you will get a short-term cash loan to help you get to the end of the month. Either an automatic deposit is set up through your bank account, or you post a check to be cashed out later in the month. When your payday rolls around, the money will automatically leave your account to pay off the loan. People usually take out a payday loans because they are struggling to make ends meet and are in some sort of financial crisis. Usually, this is because they did not plan their finances properly. I have heard horror stories of payday loans where you end up in a constant cycle of taking out new loans because you cannot pay for the previous ones. Because the interest rate is so high, you end up in such a large amount of debt that it is difficult to crawl your way out.

When it comes to bad debt, it is important to ask yourself whether or not you actually need it. There are usually other ways around the situation rather than getting yourself into a financial position that becomes very stressful. This is why there was such a big emphasis on creating a budget at the beginning of this book. When you have a budget, you are able to see how much money you have and whether or not you are able to purchase certain things. It allows you to prioritize so you don't have to get yourself into debt.

HOW TO GET OUT OF DEBT

Oh no! You've landed yourself in debt; now what? It is very possible to still end up in debt, even if you tried your best to stay out of it. Maybe there was a financial crisis, or you just didn't plan well enough. There are tons of reasons people end up in debt and struggle to pay it off. The good news is that there are always ways to get out of debt, even if you have been in it for a while. I will always say it is better to avoid it than try to resolve it. However, you shouldn't completely freak out if you do find yourself in some sort of debt. Having a plan is the most important thing when it comes to this type of situation.

Always Pay More Than the Minimum

This was highlighted in a previous chapter, but it's such an important point when it comes to paying off debt. The minimum amount that a bank or financial service provider requires you to pay for any debt you take out is basically just to cover the interest. It's not going to cover the amount you actually took the loan for. This means you can end up paying off the loan for many years into the future. This will result in you paying way more than what you actually took out. This is definitely not the best situation.

Whenever you have debt, it is a good idea to look at how much is required for the minimum. This way, you know how much you need to pay in order to be in good standing and avoid any kind of late fee. Once you have this information, you can then move on to paying more than the minimum. The more you pay into a debt, the quicker it will be paid off.

Let's say you have different types of debt. Maybe you took out a student loan, you have a credit card, and you took out a personal loan for something else. You might not have the money to pay more than the minimum on multiple types of debt and loans. Instead, just pay the minimum on all of them and pick one to pay over and above that minimum. This way, you can pay this one off quickly and then work on the next one. It doesn't have to be an overwhelming process if you take it one step at a time.

The Debt Snowball

The debt snowball is one of the best ways to get rid of all your debt. Many people have tried out this method, and it really does work because it not only helps you pay off your debt but it also works on your psychology. This means that you are more likely to pay off debt because you can see it happening in front of you. Many people struggle to pay off debt because it seems like it's never going to end. This strategy helps you develop momentum so you can get it done quickly.

For this strategy to work, you will need to know what type of debt you have and how much you owe on each type. Take some time to write out a list of all your debts. Next to the name, put the amount you owe and the minimum payments needed. Then write it out in order from the lowest amount you owe all the way to the highest amount you owe.

Now, the plan is for you to pay the minimum on all your debt. Once you have that sorted, you will move on to focusing on the smallest debt you have. You will put all your extra money into this smallest debt and pay it off as quickly as possible. Once you have completely eliminated this debt, you can cross it off the list. Then you will take all the money you were paying into the first type of debt and put it into the second type of debt. Once the second type is completely paid off, you will move on to the third and fourth, and so on.

This creates a snowball effect. If you live in an area where it snows a lot, you can do an experiment. Take a small snowball and roll it down a large hill. You will notice that when it gets to the bottom, the snowball is a lot bigger. This is because it picks up the snow and gets faster as it rolls down. This is exactly what you are doing with your debt. You are starting off with the smallest one, and as you continue paying off all the money you owe, you end up paying it off a lot faster. It is very motivating to see all your different types of debt being paid off at a consistent pace.

The Debt Avalanche

The debt snowball is not a method for everyone. Since you are only focusing on the amount you owe, you can end up paying more in interest. Remember that every single type of debt has its own interest rate. If you are only focused on the total amount, then you are not looking at the interest rate. In order to combat this, the debt avalanche method was born.

With this method, it starts off almost exactly the same as the snowball method. You will need to write down a list of all your debts and make sure you're paying the minimum on each one. However, you will need an extra piece of information. You will need to know how much interest you are paying on each type of debt. Then you will write your debt in order from the highest interest rate all the way to the lowest. The main goal is to pay off the highest interest rate first. This is so that, in the long term, you are paying a lot less. Doing this makes handling your debt a lot easier.

Once you are done handling the debt with the highest interest rate, then you can move on to the next one on the list until you've completely paid off all your debt. It will take you a bit longer to pay off your first debt because it is the biggest one. However, after this is completely handled, the other ones will be paid off very quickly. This is because you'll have a large amount of money to put into your other types of debt. It doesn't mean that you will need a bit more willpower at the beginning because it might take quite a long time to get the first one handled. If you are okay with doing this, then the debt avalanche method is the one for you.

Can You Cut Back?

Regardless of which method you decide to go for, you will need to cut back on certain areas. When you have a debt to pay off, that is going to be your main financial goal. Otherwise, it will always be the thing that holds you back from reaching your other financial goals. Having a look at your budget and seeing where you can cut back is essential. Paying off your debt means that you will have to make sacrifices in certain areas.

Perhaps you are spending too much money on food or going out. You might need to cut back for a few months just to boost your debt repayments. Looking for cheaper options will really help. For example, you can look for cheaper brands of food items, go out to free activities with your friends, and choose not to buy anything new for a few months. In fact, doing a 'no spend' challenge during this time is a great idea!

STUDENT LOANS

America is currently in a $1.6 trillion student loan crisis (Ellis, 2022). You read that right, TRILLION! That is a lot of money. It seems like almost every person who studied after school took out a student loan in order to pay for it, and now we have a major problem. The problem is that most students and even their parents are not aware of how these loans work. It becomes a future problem that you only deal with once you graduate. Even if you have just started college, graduation is just a few years away, and then you are going to be stuck paying back all this money.

If you are planning on studying further, a student loan is not your only option. It is always a good idea to know what you are getting yourself into if you are planning on taking out a loan. A loan has to always be paid back. You are just borrowing money from someone else so you can pay for your studies now. However, there is going to be an interest rate, so you will be paying back more than the amount you are borrowing. When it comes to student loans, you can use the money for things like your college tuition, study materials, and boarding. What you're paying for is not really checked by the entity that has granted you the loan, so some people misuse it. They might purchase things like a spring break trip, a new outfit, and going out to a fancy dinner. That's actually pretty scary because you can end up in a huge amount of debt and not even think about it because you're having such a good time.

One thing to note is that a student loan is not the same thing as a grant or a scholarship. With a grant or scholarship, you are not required to pay it back to the person who is paying for your studies. You might need to agree to work for a company in order to get a scholarship, but you do not need to physically pay back any money. It is a bit more difficult to get a grant or scholarship since these are usually very competitive and a private company gets to decide who gets them and who doesn't. However, it is definitely worth it to apply for as many as possible so you do not have to worry about taking out a student loan.

When applying to colleges, you would also be given a federal student aid application. On this form, follow the prompts and fill out the financial details of both you and your parents. Each of your potential schools will take this information and work out how much financial aid you would qualify for. After that, you will get a letter that shows you how much financial aid you can get and all the details about it. In some cases, the financial aid could come through a scholarship or grant and not a student loan. It is always a good idea to fill out this form because you do have the opportunity to get a scholarship or grant, but just make sure that you don't blindly accept any offer that is given to you.

Another option is to apply for a private student loan, which does not go through the federal government. The private company that is offering the loan will stipulate how much needs to be paid back and by when. Regardless of whether you are taking out a federal student loan or a private one, you will have to sign a document that promises you will pay back the money at a later date. This means that you are already in debt before landing your first serious job. This is why student loans are so scary.

There are a few things that are important to know about when it comes to student loans. There might be words flying around that you simply have no idea about, and it can get very confusing. The three things that are most important to consider when it comes to your student loan are the loan repayment term, the interest rate, and the principal.

The loan repayment term is just how long you have until you need to pay back the loan in full. You won't have to pay any money while you are still studying, but as soon as you graduate and get your first job, you will need to start paying back your loan. When it comes to private loans, the company that issues the loan will decide exactly how long you have to pay it back. This will be in the agreement you sign when you take out the loan. When it comes to federal loans, it is usually about 10 years, but some can be increased to 20 or even 30 years.

We have already spoken about interest rates in a previous chapter, so you probably have a good idea of what this is. The interest rate will vary depending on where you got the loan and the terms in the contract. In most cases, you will get a fixed interest rate, but this is not always the case. You might also get a rate based on your or your parent's credit rating, so you might be able to get a better rate if you have a good credit score. This is especially true when it comes to private student loans.

The principal is the amount that you would initially be taking out. So if you need $20,000 in order to study, you will take this out at the beginning. However, this amount definitely increases based on the interest rate. By the time you are ready to start making payments, you owe a lot more than $20,000.

Your Loan Responsibility After College

So let's fast forward a few years, and now you have graduated from college. You've got your degree, and you've landed your first job. You quickly realize that you do not earn as much as you would have liked, and that means you can't commit to making all the payments on your student loan. What now? A major problem when it comes to student loans is that you never know what type of job or career you'll be walking into after you graduate from college. There are many different circumstances that could impact your income and job. But now you have made a commitment to pay back a certain amount every month until the loan is paid off in full. You're basically making a promise for your future that you might not be able to keep.

If you are unable to afford your payments, there are a few things you can do. None of them are particularly ideal, but there are some options. For one, you can put the payment on hold until you get to a place where you can afford to continue paying. The problem with this is that your loan will continue to increase in interest. You'll have to go directly to the company or agency that has given you your loan and speak to them about this option. By the time you unfreeze the payments, you might owe a whole lot more on your loan.

Another option is to defer payment for a short time. Depending on the financial institution that is giving you your loan, you might not need to pay interest. But this being said, you do have to be eligible for a deferment option to take place. This might not be something that is available to you, so make sure you have done your research and are aware.

Another option is to have your loan forgiven, but again, not everyone has this option available to them. You might need to do some public service, like work at a low-income school for a certain number of years or work for the government. These jobs will not pay very well, but at least you will be able to have your student loan forgiven. With this being said, there are a very small number of people who can get their student loans forgiven. Applications are denied all the time for various reasons, so this is not a reliable way to go about removing a student loan. Even though there has been a lot of talk in the news recently about expanding student loan forgiveness, it is a hot political football and certainly not something you should count on.

The next option is to refinance your loan. This can be a very confusing topic, but it's when you take your current loan and turn it into a brand-new loan. You still must pay back the money, but the terms are different. You can only refinance through a private company or lender, and it cannot be done through government or federal support. However, you can refinance a federal loan through a private lender. Basically, you will go to your private lender and get them to pay off your current student loan. You will no longer owe the old lender but will now be in a new agreement with a new lender. There will be new terms for you to pay back the loan. If you have taken out many different student loans, you can combine all of them into one loan through refinancing. This can be a great option, but make sure you are getting a good deal. It should be free to refinance your current loans, and you should also look for a lower interest rate. There are many scammers out there; just make sure you are not caught off guard.

Let's say none of these options work for you, and you end up missing a ton of payments. If you must make just one payment, it probably won't be that bad. You will likely get a notice from your loan provider, and you might need to pay a fee. If you are able to get back on track and continue making your regular payments, everything should be fine. However, this is not always the case, and if you miss quite a few payments, you might end up defaulting. This means that you have not kept up your end of the bargain and now must face some consequences for this. Depending on the actions your loan provider takes, you might end up in court or be required to pay your entire amount immediately. It basically becomes a huge mess that is difficult to work your way around. It is always better not to get yourself into this type of situation. You might need a financial advisor or a debt counselor to help you through this so you can get a solid plan in place.

How to Possibly Avoid Student Loans

Now that you have all of this knowledge, you might be thinking that a student loan is not a great option for you. I would always suggest exploring all of your options and making a student loan your last resort. If you are currently in school and thinking of going to college in a few years, this is the perfect time for you to think about how you're going to finance that responsibility. Racking up $100K in student loan debt to end up with a job that pays $40K/yr. is a recipe for disaster. As a young teen living with your parents, $40k/yr. may sound like a lot of money, but once you break out on your own and handle all your own expenses, you will quickly learn that it is not.

It would be helpful to come up with a few different career paths that might interest you. Then do an internet search to see what the pay range is for jobs in that field. From here, you can decide on what areas of the country you may want to live in and try to calculate what a livable wage is in that area. This will give you a better idea if it is a good career choice and if you will make enough in the area you choose.

Your first point of call should be to look for scholarships and grants. If you are a few years away from applying to college, you can look at what the stipulations are in order to get certain scholarships and grants. Some require high academic achievement, and others will require you to have lots of extracurricular activities. If you know what is required to get one of these scholarships or grants, then you can make a plan to do that now. It will make your application a lot more attractive, and you will have a higher chance of landing financial aid.

You should also do some deep research into the type of college or university you want to attend. Not all of them are made equal, and some charge incredibly high prices that are completely unnecessary. You should go to a school that you can actually afford. Sometimes public universities and community colleges get a bad reputation. People always aim to go to the best and most expensive Ivy League schools. However, this is usually not necessary, as your education can be just as good at a cheaper school or university. Have a look at the courses available at a community college or a public university. Compare the prices here to a private university. You will quickly see that there is a massive difference in the amount you're going to pay. You could also go to the community college for a year or two before transferring over to a more prestigious school. Doing the core courses here will make it a lot cheaper for you, and you can still get your degree from your chosen college.

It is also worth looking at schools in your state and ones that you can commute to. I know all the college movies show people having an amazing time when they stay on campus and in sororities. Many teenagers dream of the day they can move out of their parents' house and have the true college experience. But this college experience is not the point of going to college. The point is to graduate with a degree so you can set yourself up for the future. You can still have many awesome experiences and make great friends even if you don't stay on campus. If your parents are willing to let you stay at home while you study, this can really cut down on costs. You don't have to pay for any living expenses, and you won't need to think about things like food or laundry either.

Once you have done all of that research and really thought about what you are going to college for, you can start saving up for it. It doesn't matter what your age is; you can never be too young to start saving up for your education. Getting a part-time job or even doing some freelance work if you are particularly skilled in a certain area can be a great way for you to make some extra money. You can save all of this money in a savings account and use it when you graduate and are ready to go to college. If you are already in college, don't let that stop you from trying to get a job. You can get an off-campus job and use the money to pay for college, or you can get an on-campus job where you can get discounts on your college tuition. There might be work-study programs at your college where you can become a teaching assistant or work on campus in some capacity. You might not get paid a whole lot, but they will contribute towards your study fees. Another bonus is that you will have something to add to your resume when you graduate. Any work experience is amazing when you're looking for a job after college.

The final thing you can do to cut down on costs and avoid student loans is to keep it cheap. This just means that you don't have to blow a whole bunch of money to have a good college experience. Don't get sucked into the party lifestyle or spend so much just to look cool. It's really not worth it, and besides, after you graduate, you are probably never going to see most of those people again. Remember to create a budget and then stick to it as closely as possible. This will also help you when you graduate and get your first job because you will know how to manage your money.

Explore Other Avenues

When it comes to preparing for a career, many people don't even need to go to a four-year college. There are so many different paths that can land you in a good, high-paying job that is so much cheaper than a four-year college. You should think about what you are studying to become rather than just focusing on getting into a college. Sure, becoming a doctor or lawyer does make college a necessity, but many other careers do not require it. For example, trade schools are amazing alternatives because you can get into a trade career and still make a really good salary. On top of that, you will finish studying earlier and won't have all the debt to pay back. A career in a trade such as plumbing or welding can far out pay a career landed with a traditional degree. Here are a few more examples of high-paying jobs that don't require a degree:

- Licensed Nurse
- Carpenter
- Real Estate Agent
- Electrician
- Sales Representatives

- Detectives and Police Officers
- Dental Hygienist
- Air Traffic Controller
- Web Developer

With these jobs, some education is necessary, but you will hit the job market way sooner and start building your career. This means you can climb the ladder and have the advantage of professional work experience. If starting your own business is a goal of yours, this might be an easier path for you. In most of the jobs listed above, you can venture into your own business after a few years of working. This means even more earning potential. Remember, you don't have to follow a certain path because it seems like the most popular one. Think about what you really want to do with your life and look for the best way to get there. This will allow you to make smart decisions that lead to a happier and more successful life.

ACTIVITY: PLAY PAYBACK

Many students think the only thing that will get them into debt is their tuition fees. This is actually not the case. When you go to college, there are going to be plenty of things you need to pay for. Follow this link and play the payback game: www.timeforpayback.com.

This is going to take you through your college years as a simulation. It will help you understand exactly how much debt you might end up with based on your decisions. It will help you play multiple times and make different choices to see the outcomes.

ACTIVITY: CLAIM YOUR FUTURE

Claim Your Future: fame.claimyourfuture.org/student-registration is another great game you can play online. It will help you explore the different career choices you will have as you get older. Try it out and see the results.

6

GROW YOUR WEALTH

When Justin was 13 years old, he figured out the wonders of the stock market. There was just something interesting about watching how your money could grow or even plummet in the space of a few minutes or days. He took some time to research the stock market and how it worked. In fact, for his 14th birthday, he asked his parents to get him a subscription to an investment site. This is where he learned a lot about the stock market and investing in general. He would read articles upon articles on the subject, and eventually, he decided he wanted to make his own investment.

His first investment wasn't a big one, and he had randomly chosen the company he wanted to invest in.

Basically, he was chomping down on a delicious donut from Dunkin' Donuts and decided that it was a good company to invest in. After he made his investment, he saw the increase in a few weeks. This was incredibly exciting for him, and he decided that this is something he wants to continue doing. He spoke to his parents, and they were willing to help him through his investments. Eventually, his Dunkin' Donuts stock tanked because he got a bit too confident with it. He made a couple of other bad investments because he was overly confident with the first Dunkin' Donuts investment. After that, he learned a valuable lesson about not investing with your emotions. Now that he is older, he is so much better at investing and it is something that he does to supplement his current income.

It is many years later, and he always thinks back to the time when he first started investing. He has definitely learned some lessons from that point, but those were so valuable. Now that he's older, he has a very solid investment strategy that is actually making him money. He remembers not to get greedy and to do his research before any investment.

Now I have a question for you. Do you know the difference between investing and saving? A lot of times, these two subjects are used interchangeably. We can talk about saving for the future and investing for the future, so what exactly is the difference? Well, when it comes to saving, you are putting away money for the future. If you save $100 now, you will have $100 in 10 years' time. Investing is like one step above saving. The goal is to invest in something that's going to make you more money in the long run. So if you invest $100 today, you would hope to have $1000 in 10 years.

WHAT IS INVESTING?

When you invest, you are taking an action that can allow your money to grow over a certain period of time. Some investments are passive and others are active. A passive investment is something that you put your money into and then leave it to grow by itself. You don't really need to do much in order for your investment to increase. An active investment is something that you invest in, but you also need to take action. For example, running your own business would be a form of active investing because you're putting your money into your business but you also must run it so you can continue making a profit.

There is a fine line between active and passive investing. Since there are so many different ways you can invest, you might find ways to actively invest in something that is traditionally a passive investment. When it comes to these types of investments, there isn't really a right or wrong answer. However, it is a good idea to have a few passive investments. If you find ways to make money without doing much, you will be able to grow your wealth. Who doesn't want to become rich and not have to do a lot of work at the same time?

When you are trying to make an investment, you should always look at the return on your investment. This is also known as the ROI. It shows how well your investment could potentially perform and how much profit you can get from it. Whenever you get a benefit or an income from an investment, it is called a return. You can work out your ROI by yourself and then get a percentage. Here is the formula:

ROI = Cost of Investment / Current Value of Investment – Cost of Investment

When you use this formula, you'll be able to see whether you're going to get a profit or loss from your investment. Since this is a percentage, you will also be able to rank different investment options so you can see which ones are the best. The higher the ROI, the better for you. Just remember that this is not entirely accurate because there are many different factors when it comes to investing. I wish it was just as simple as this, but in the real world, there are so many things that can impact how well or how badly an investment can do. And also, it just gives you a good base point to look at whether or not it has the potential of being a good investment.

When it comes to investing, you should always start as early as possible. I know investing can seem like something only fully grown and well-established adults should do, but this is definitely not the case. If you have money, then you should try your hand at investing. You might need the help of an adult in order to get started but do your best to make your own decisions. You can do research to find the various types of investments you can make. Once you start investing, you will get a good feel for how it works. It is all well and good to have all the information in front of you, but there's no replacement for practicing on your own.

When it comes to investing, time is so important. The longer you have your investments, the more opportunities they have to grow. Many people wait a very long time before they start investing. This means they have to invest more in order to get the amount they want. If you can start investing at a younger age, you will be ahead of so many people and will likely be able to make a lot more money through investing. You can start with smaller investments and then work your way up. There are many different types of investments that don't even need a lot of money for you to get started.

The Different Types

The great thing about investing is that there are so many different options available. Every person is different, and that means one investment strategy is not going to work for everyone. Knowing the different types of investments can help you narrow down which ones you want to try out.

Stocks and Bonds

Stocks and bonds are by far the most popular investment types out there. These are two different types of investments, but they're usually lumped into one. Let's first talk about stocks. A stock is a share or a part of a company. When a company wants to grow, it needs money to do so. What they will do is sell a part of the company on the stock market. Investors can purchase these stocks, and the company will make money from them. The company can use this to expand and increase profits. As the company grows, its value will also increase. This means the stock on the stock market will increase in value as well. The investors buy and then sell their stock for a higher price than what they paid for it. Now they will make a profit from the stock they originally purchased.

Another way you can make money through stocks is by purchasing a dividend stock. Not every stock on the stock market is a dividend stock, so you need to just check to make sure. Companies that offer dividend stocks are typically more established. When you purchase a dividend stock, you will be able to make money in the traditional way, as discussed above, but you will also get paid out in dividends. A dividend is a portion of the profit a company makes in a certain time frame. You can get paid out for your dividend quarterly, bi-annually, or annually. It all depends on the company.

Even though stocks and bonds are usually referred to together, a bond is very different from a stock. When you take out a bond, you are actually becoming someone who loans a company or government money. A company or the government might need money to grow in a certain area or for whatever else they need. You will then make money through interest earned throughout the duration of the bond. Basically, this is the opposite of when you take out a loan. The roles are reversed. You must commit to a bond for a certain amount of time, and once the time is up, you will get paid back the amount you lent out plus the interest. At this point, it is called a bond maturity date.

A bond is typically a much safer investment option than a stock. Unless the company you have loaned money to completely goes under, you are pretty much guaranteed to get your money back. Government bonds are even more secure than company ones. When it comes to stocks in the stock market, it can be quite volatile. Volatile means that the prices on the stock market are constantly moving up and down. One day the price doubles; the next it could plummet all the way down, but then suddenly the next day it's back up again. This means that a stock is a riskier investment than a bond. With this being said, a stock also has the potential for a higher reward. Stocks tend to make investors a lot more money if you are able to pick the right stocks and the right strategy.

It is usually best to balance out your investment portfolio by investing in both stocks and bonds. One of the biggest mistakes an investor can make is to just invest in one thing. All investments are quite risky, so it really matters to diversify your portfolio. If you do a mixture of stocks and bonds, then you can balance out the safety and security of a bond as well as the potential growth of a stock. This is usually how people invest, so they get the best of both worlds.

Funds

A fund is a great way to invest if you aren't really interested in making all the investments yourself. It takes a lot of knowledge and planning to invest and make sure you are investing in the right things. Not only that, but it can take quite a lot of time to sit down and make the investment. If this is not something you want to do, then a fund is a great option.

There are very different funds that you can invest in. The most popular are mutual funds and exchange-traded funds. When you invest in a fund, you get a signed investment manager. This person will take the investment money of multiple different investors and invest it in stocks and bonds. The portfolio manager will do their best to invest safely and in a way that's going to make the most money for the investors. All you must do is pay a monthly premium to your portfolio manager and the company they work for. This premium will include the amount you will be investing each month as well as the fees that you need to pay to have your fund managed.

Since the investment manager has a much larger amount of money to work with, they can invest a lot more. This means the potential for an increase is higher. This is a great way to make a passive income because you really don't have to do much. You can communicate with your fund manager about your goals and what you need to accomplish with your investment fund. This will help the investor know where and how to invest. You will also be able to track your investments, so you are not going to be completely in the dark about what is going on.

Retirement Plans

A retirement fund is a way for people to save towards their retirement in a safe and secure way. These also have tax benefits, which many other investment funds don't have. The most popular retirement plans are IRAs and 401(k)s. These work slightly differently, but they are both great for investing in your future retirement.

An IRA stands for an individual retirement account. Any person can open up an IRA and start investing their money in it for their retirement. There are two types of IRAs: the traditional IRA and the Roth IRA. With a traditional IRA, you will not need to pay tax on any of the contributions you make. Then, when it comes time for you to withdraw from your account, you will pay tax based on the rate at that point. This helps you save on taxes right now. Then you have the

Roth IRA, in which you pay tax on your contributions now but not when you withdraw later on. Since tax rates are likely to increase over time, a Roth IRA is a great option to save money in the long term and make sure that you're not held down by taxes when you are older.

A 401(k) is a retirement account that is given to you by your employer. Not all employers will deposit into a 401(k), but if you work for a company that does, you should definitely take advantage of this. With a 401(k), both you and your employer will be contributing to the account. In many cases, they will match your contributions. So if you decide that you want to invest $200, your employer will match that and also contribute $200. So your total contributions for the month will be $400. In some cases, your employer will work on a percentage basis, so you will have to contribute a percentage rather than a specific dollar amount. Either way, you are getting free money in your retirement account. It is always a good idea to check with your employer to see how much they are willing to match. There is usually a limit to the matching amount, and if you can, you should max this out. This means that if your employer is willing to match your contributions up to $500, you should do your best to invest $500 as well. This way, you can double up on your retirement investing and make sure that when you are older, you have the retirement of your dreams.

You can also open multiple retirement accounts. If you have a 401(k) through your employer, you could also open up an IRA for additional retirement investing. This is completely up to you, but make sure you don't open up too many different accounts. This can make it difficult for you to grow your investments if they are split all over the place. In most cases, you would also be able to take your retirement account from one employer to the next, so make sure you find out all of these things if you are looking to change jobs in the future.

Cryptocurrencies

Another type of investment that has become popular recently is cryptocurrency. You might see people talking about this all the time on social media. It's actually a very interesting topic and something that we should keep an eye on. One thing to note about cryptocurrency is that it is incredibly unstable. Since it is a new type of investment, there is no guarantee that it will withstand the long term. This means that if you want to invest in cryptocurrency, you can, but you shouldn't make it your main source of investment or invest all your money in it. There are people who have made a ton of money through investing in cryptocurrency, but there have also been people who have lost it all.

Other

In this category, there are plenty of different types of investments. There are tons of things that can qualify. One of these things is a commodity. These are tangible investments, such as agriculture, metals, life stock, and even energy in the form of oil or gas. It can be very difficult to invest in commodities because changes in the political climate can make a huge shift in this area. If you are investing in things like agriculture, if there is a weather problem, that could affect your investment as well. A person who invests in commodities needs to understand the future of the market as well as many different areas that could impact their investment.

Other forms of investment could include buying things like art. Typically, the price of art does increase over time if you buy the right pieces. Art collectors are able to purchase and hold their pieces for a long time before they decide to sell it for a profit. This type of investment really does require you to have complete knowledge of the market. It's definitely not something you should invest in as a beginner because it's going to cost you a lot of money and you don't really know if the artist is going to be someone valuable in the future. Gold and other precious metals could also be good investments. In most cases, this does increase in price over time and become more valuable.

GETTING STARTED

Now that you know the different types of investments out there and what investing actually is, it's time for you to get started. Getting started with investing as early as possible is an amazing opportunity. Even just learning about investments at a younger age gives you a chance to be a step ahead.

Before you start investing your actual money, you must figure out what your investment style is. This just means you need to know how much time and money you are going to be giving towards your investments. As you get older, your investment style is probably going to change. This is likely because you'll have more or less time as well as more or less money. Besides this, there are lots of things that could impact your investment style. For example, your personality and how much time you are willing to spend on research. At the end of the day, you need to be happy with your investments because it's something that you are going to do in the long term. If you can't keep up with the type of investments that you are looking into, then it's really not going to be worth it to start.

You also want to take into consideration your budget. As a teenager, you might not have access to thousands of dollars to start investing. Before you start investing, you need to have enough in your savings account to keep you going if there are any emergencies. It is always a big mistake to invest before you have some sort of savings or emergency fund. This is because most investments are not accessible quickly. You usually must lock down your investments, or you might need to take them out if you are hit with an emergency, which may be the wrong time.

Once you have some funds tucked away for an emergency, you can start including investing in your budget. You really don't want to pick up and sell all your investments every single time your car needs to go to the mechanic, you need medication, or some other small issue pops up. Remember to work your investment into your budget so you know exactly how much you are able to invest each month. Investing should be a habit that you build consistently.

The final thing you want to consider when you are thinking about what you are going to invest in is your risk tolerance. This is an essential part of investing because every investment has a different level of risk. Most people are not happy taking any risk when it comes to money, but this is unrealistic. I have already mentioned that stocks tend to be risky investments because of their volatility. However, with the risk comes the potential to make a lot more money. This is usually how it is with most investments. The more risks you take, the more opportunities you must make more money. However, this also means there is a higher potential to lose a lot of money. A risk is a balancing act.

Not everybody has a high-risk tolerance. Some people get incredibly nervous when they make risky investments. If you cannot handle a lot of risks, then it is usually better for you to play it safe. There are other factors that come into play when talking about how much risk you can take. For example, somebody who is older will have a lower risk tolerance. If you are 20 years old, when you start investing, you can take out a risky investment but end up losing it all. You have more time to make up for it. You have a solid 40 to 50 years to invest and make back your money. However, if you are 50 years old and you only have 10 years until you retire, then it is not a good idea to make a risky investment. If you end up losing your money, then you will not have enough time to make it back.

As a younger person, you definitely have a lot more options in terms of your investment because you have the time to play around and see what's going to work for you. When it comes to your investment strategy, sometimes you are going to have to try out a ton of different things before you decide what's going to work best for you.

OPENING A BROKERAGE ACCOUNT (WITH PARENTS)

Many investments will not be accessible to you as a teenager because you will need the help of an adult. This just means you must rope your parents into helping you create your investment account. An investment account is often called a brokerage account because you will need the help of a broker to invest your money.

As a teenager, you and your parents can open something called a custodial brokerage account. Other family members, including grandparents, can also open an account for you if you are still a minor. Once you turn 18 or 21 years old, the account will be transferred to you completely. You have full control over it and all the money that's in the account. With these kinds of accounts, you do own everything that is in the account, even when you are under the age of 18. It's just that you do not have access to it without the help of your parents. This also means that if you are liable for capital gains tax, this will be in your name and not the adult who helped you open the account.

When looking for a broker, you should look for one that offers a custodial account with very little to no account fees and a minimum deposit requirement. This way, you are able to start investing even if you don't have a lot of money. The most common options for investment accounts for teenagers are a custodial standard brokerage account or a Roth IRA. You can open these accounts pretty easily online, and it shouldn't take you more than 20 minutes to do. Just make sure you have all the necessary information on hand. You'll be able to find out what information and documentation you need if you go to your financial service provider's website.

Once you've opened your account, you can start making investments. This means you can start investing in stocks, which can be really exciting. Remember to do your research and pick the ones you believe are going to grow with time. It is often the most exhilarating when you choose a stock from a company that you are passionate about and that you really like. Once you have chosen a few individual stocks, you can build your investment portfolio with funds as well.

Index, mutual, and ETFs are great funds to put in your investment portfolio. This will help you diversify your investment so it's not just stuck on one thing. It's also much easier to keep track of your investments if they are all in one fund.

After you have made all of your investments, the journey doesn't end there. You still need to track all of your investments to make sure they are performing well. Things always change when it comes to investing. Sometimes things are good, and sometimes things are bad. In some cases, you'll need to make changes, and in others, you can just let your investments do their thing. However, it's important to make a habit of checking your investments, so if there are changes that need to be made, you can make them as soon as possible.

ACTIVITY: WOULD YOU RATHER

Here's a cool question: Would you rather be given $1 million in cash or be given a penny and double it every day for a month?

This might seem quite silly because who is going to choose the penny? However, there is something surprising that happens when you start doubling your money. Here's what I want you to do: Start doubling the penny for 30 days and see how much you end up with. I promise you are going to be surprised and might want to change your mind if you choose the $1 million.

Day 1	$0.02	Day 16	
Day 2	$0.04	Day 17	
Day 3		Day 18	
Day 4		Day 19	
Day 5		Day 20	
Day 6		Day 21	
Day 7		Day 22	
Day 8		Day 23	
Day 9		Day 24	
Day 10		Day 25	
Day 11		Day 26	
Day 12		Day 27	
Day 13		Day 28	
Day 14		Day 29	
Day 15		Day 30	

ACTIVITY: RETURN ON INVESTMENT

Using the ROI formula that you learned above, answer the below questions:

- Jasper bought a share in Starbucks for $33.38. He decided to sell it five years later at the closing price of $6.09. What was his return on investment?
- Leah also bought Starbucks stock on the same day Jasper did. She sold it six years later at a

closing price of $34.38. What was her return on investment?

- Marcus bought 10 shares of Apple stock for $275.33. Three years later, he sold it for $667.38 per share. What was his return on investment?

7

BOOST YOUR INCOME

If you think that building a business or making your own money is something only adults can do, then think again. There are so many kids and teenagers who started their own businesses and became incredibly successful. One of these young people's names is Bella Tipping, and she started her business when she was just 12 years old. Bella and her family loved going on a family vacation, but she felt that she wasn't having as much fun as she could have. Many times her parents would book vacations, and even though the adults had a good time, the kids didn't really have that much to do. She wanted to have vacations she could remember and enjoy with her siblings as well.

This is when she came up with the idea for Kidzcationz. This is a platform where kids can get advice on different vacation spots based on their own experiences. If you've ever used a website like Tripadvisor, where you can type in a restaurant or holiday destination to find out whether it's good or not, then you would have a pretty good idea of what Bella's website does. It's a place where all children's opinions can be heard based on what they experience on their vacations. It was made even more kid-friendly because it doesn't use the names and faces of the kids but instead uses avatars.

Her parents saw how passionate she was about this, so she developed a business plan. This business plan outlined exactly how much money she would need and how she planned to grow the business. After this, her parents were very supportive, and they knew that she was serious so they invested a huge chunk of money to see the business grow.

Bella saw a gap in the market that needed to be filled. It was a need, and she was willing to find a solution to not only make her life more comfortable but also the lives of many other children. There are tons of ways that younger people can start businesses and find creative ways to make money for themselves. You can be one of these stories as well.

TEEN ENTREPRENEUR

Let's first discuss what an entrepreneur is. It's a pretty big word, but it basically means starting and running your own business. When you run your own business, you become an entrepreneur. You are the one making all the decisions and taking on most of the risk, but you are also enjoying the majority of the rewards that come with it. I don't want to lie to you; building your own business is a lot of hard work. It's also a lot of trial and error. However, if you are able to build a successful business, it is all worth it.

Entrepreneurship is incredibly important to the economy of every country. There needs to be new businesses starting all the time in order to keep pushing forward and bringing more money into various areas and sectors. New businesses mean new ideas and innovations. As a society, we need people who are willing to take that step and start their own businesses.

If you want to start a successful business, you need to create a service or product that people actually need. One of the biggest mistakes people make when they start a business is that they just do whatever they want. It is true that passion is important when you start a business, but if there's nobody to buy your product or service, then you aren't going to be that successful. This is why doing market research is so important. Like in the story with Bella, she saw a gap in the market and created a solution to the problem. Think about the people who will be using your product or service and what annoys them or what problems they're facing. Then you can start thinking about solutions you know they will love.

It is also a good idea to get in contact with people who could potentially help you run and start your business. Even if you are the main entrepreneur in your business, you will need other people to help support you. Maybe you will need suppliers or investors, or maybe you just need some advice. A good place to start is to connect with as many entrepreneurs and business-minded people on social media as you can. These people post amazing content that you can follow and get tips and tricks from. Then look in your circle to see if there are any adults who run their own businesses. You can connect with them and ask them to have a meeting with you so you can get some ideas and advice.

Once you have it done, you also need to focus on your finances. Almost every business requires some sort of startup capital. You don't need to have all the money necessary to build up your business from the start, but you do need to have some. Try saving up as much as you can for your business so that when you are ready to start building it, you have the money to do so. You can also start creating a business pitch or plan so you can start promoting your business to investors. If you need other people to buy into your idea and give you money, then you need to show them why. Make sure you have a clear vision for your business and highlight the potential for profit as well as what you are willing to do to grow it.

Building a business and becoming an entrepreneur is a learning experience. Even when you have already established your business, it is still important that you continue to grow and learn. You can do this by reading the right books and signing up for courses that can help you in this area. The more business-minded you are, the better it's going to be for you. You will be able to think about things in a very different way and create new strategies and ideas based on what you have learned. We live in a world where information is very easily accessible, so you can find good content quite cheaply, or even for free. Subscribe to podcasts, YouTube channels, and other social media pages that speak to the areas you want to work in. The more your business and entrepreneurship are on your mind, the more you will grow.

Small Business Ideas

There are literally thousands of business ideas out there. It's up to you to pick one that you know will work for you. Everyone has different gifts and skill sets, so look at what you are good at and start from there. As a teenager, you'll probably need to find something that you can do part-time because you'll have to focus on school. Remember not to overcommit yourself; otherwise, it's going to be very difficult to balance your school and home life with your business. With this being said, every business requires you to put in effort and work in order to get it off the ground.

Photography and Videography

If you are great at taking videos and photographs, why not turn it into a business? There are tons of people who are looking for professionals to take great-quality pictures and videos for them. This could be product photography or personal photography. You'll just need the right equipment to start. In most cases, you won't be able to use your phone, as this isn't too professional.

Tutoring

If you are good at a particular skill or subject, then you can look into tutoring as a business. Most people believe they can only tutor if it is a school subject, but this is not really the case. You can do lessons in music or art if you are really good at it. Just make sure to market yourself and get the word out there that you do give lessons and are willing to teach whatever skill you have. Remember to do some research on how much you should be charging, as over or undercharging is not ideal.

House and Pet Sitting

People are always looking for reliable pet and house sitters. You can actually start a business doing this and get other teenagers to pet-sit and house-sit for you. If you are running a business, you will be the person that people contact to find reliable pet and house sitters. You will have to pay the teenagers who do the job, and you will get a cut from organizing everything. You can start off by doing it yourself, and as your business grows, you can look into adding more people.

Social Media

Social media is a great way to earn some extra money if you are a great content creator. If you don't want to earn money through your own content, you can become a social media marketer or manager. This is somebody who posts on social media for another person or company. Essentially, you'll be creating content for someone else. Eventually, you can grow this into a bigger business. Just make sure you give it your all and are creative when it comes to the ideas that you are using for your social media campaigns.

Illustrator/Designer

If you are a creative person who enjoys drawing and designing, you can become an illustrator or designer. Now that we can do all of these things in a digital format, it becomes a lot easier for you to find clients. Going to freelancing websites to look for clients is a great way to start. Then, once you have your clients, you can do the work for them to get your name out there.

Gardening

Gardening and landscaping are also great ways to make some extra cash and start a business. If you do the work well, more people will come to you for their landscaping and gardening needs. You can start this type of business in your neighborhood. Go around and ask your neighbors if anyone needs help with their gardens and show them what you're willing to do. If more and more people show interest in your gardening services, then you can hire other people to help you with the work.

These are just a few of the ideas that you can try. There are so many different types of businesses out there, so if you have an idea, you can give it a shot and see if it works. Just remember to put in as much effort and work as possible so you can get your business off the ground.

GETTING A JOB

Running your own business is definitely a great thing to do, but not everybody wants to be an entrepreneur. Some people want to get a job and work for a company, and that is completely okay. It is also a good idea to get a job while you are still working on your business ideas. This way, you can build connections with other people and earn some money to save for your business.

There are many places that hire teenagers for part-time or full-time work. A great place to start is online since the application process is pretty easy. You will just follow the prompts online until you submit your application for review. Try to look for job opportunities that align with your values and what you actually enjoy doing. This way, you have a high likelihood of enjoying your work and sticking with it for a longer time frame.

Whenever you are looking for a job, it is essential to create a resume. A resume is simply a piece of paper or a document that shows your skills and experience. If you had a job before, then you can highlight what you did at that job as well as the skills you got from doing it. If you haven't had a job before, then you can highlight other things like your skills, hobbies, and responsibilities in other areas. If you volunteer or are part of a club or sports team, you can add that to your resume. As you continue on with your career, you will add more and more information to your resume.

Once you have applied and handed out your resume, you'll have to wait until the company reaches out to you to come in for an interview. Once you have received an interview invitation, it is time to start preparing. Do your research on the company as well as the job role so that you can answer any questions they have. They might ask you why you want the job and what skills and talents you can bring to the company. Remember to be confident when you are in an interview. Since they have called you into an interview, they already liked your resume, and now they are looking to see if they like you as a person and if you are going to be a good fit for their company. Remember to listen to what they have to say and take a few seconds to pause before answering any questions they have. At the end, the interviewer will generally ask if you have any questions. Take this opportunity to ask if they see any reason why you would not be the ideal candidate for the job. This forces the interviewer to reveal any weaknesses they feel you may have, which gives you the opportunity to address those concerns.

Once the interview is done, say goodbye to each person on your interview panel and thank them for the opportunity. Make sure you get their business cards with their contact information. Then once you get home, you can email them and thank them for the opportunity and re-emphasize why you are the best fit for the job. If you have not heard back from the company in a few weeks, you can call or email them to ask for feedback. This way, you are always on their mind and have a higher chance of landing a job with them. If you don't get a job, remember that it is not the end of the world. Use this as a learning opportunity, and think about how you can improve for the next interview. You should always apply for multiple jobs at a time because you don't know which one is going to actually work out for you. The more choices you have, the better for you.

UNDERSTANDING TAXATION

Taxes are probably something you have heard many adults talk about, and usually they are complaining. But what exactly are taxes, and how do they impact you? Well, when you get a job and earn a certain amount of money, you will need to pay taxes. This is money that you pay to the government so you can benefit from public services and spaces. There are lots of different types of taxes, such as income tax, property tax, sales tax, and capital gains tax. The government needs that money since it is their main and sometimes only source of income.

Income tax is the tax that you pay on your income. When you make money through your business or your job, you'll have to pay income tax. Sales tax is what is added to items at the store. Capital gains tax is the tax you pay on your assets and your investments. Property tax is the tax that you pay on any property that you own. Companies and individuals all have to pay taxes in these various areas.

Being a citizen of a country means you are obligated to pay tax if you earn more than a certain amount of money. It is actually illegal to avoid being taxed, and you can end up paying huge fees or even going to jail. Tax evasion is a serious crime, and even celebrities get caught doing it (just ask Shakira). This is why it is better to make sure all your taxes are paid up so you can avoid any of these negative consequences.

Typically, you will pay your taxes annually. The exception to this is sales tax, which is paid as soon as you purchase an item from the shop. When you pay your taxes annually, you will need to make sure you have all your documents in order. This means you need to know exactly how much you made in the year and what your tax rate is. There are certain things that will help lower the amount of tax you pay. This will be different based on where you live. For example, if you have a retirement account, you might be able to pay less taxes if you have a tax-deferred account like a traditional IRA. Donations to certain organizations can also lower the amount of tax you pay.

At the end of a tax year, which is not the same as a regular year, you'll have to fill out all your tax forms. You can easily find out when the tax year ends by typing it into your search engine. This will help you prepare well in advance. If you aren't earning any money, you don't have to worry about paying taxes. However, it is always a good idea to find out what the tax threshold is in your area. If you do not pay taxes for one year, it does not disappear. It gets carried over, and late fees are added. This means you might need to pay a lot more money. It is better to stay on top of things. If you are not confident with this, there are many tax services that can complete this whole process for you.

ACTIVITY: INTERVIEWING AN ENTREPRENEUR

If you are looking to become a business owner or an entrepreneur, then interviewing one is going to be so valuable. You probably know one or two people who have started their own business. If you don't, you can ask your parents if they know someone. Set up an interview either in person or through a video call. Then get ready to ask them some questions. This will help you understand what they actually do and what is required to be an entrepreneur. You can ask any questions you want, but here are some ideas:

- What does an average day in your life look like?
- How did you come up with your business idea, and what inspired you?
- What challenges did you face when you first started out?
- What advice would you give me as I am trying to become an entrepreneur?
- What do you think are the most important qualities of a good entrepreneur?
- Is there anything you would have done differently based on what you know now?

ACTIVITY: WHICH JOBS ALIGN WITH MY INTEREST?

Thinking about what you want to do for the rest of your life could be very overwhelming, but we all start somewhere. The good news is that there are so many different types of jobs out there that you are probably going to find one that you really enjoy and aligns with your interests and personality. What you need to do is take some time to really think about it. Fill out the below tables to help you narrow down what kinds of jobs could be great options for you.

Jobs I Love!	Jobs I Hate!

Have a look at the above and see if there are any similarities on each list. Think about why you have listed certain jobs under the love category and others under the hate category. You might notice there are a few things that make a job more or less attractive to you. Now that you have this information, you can avoid certain jobs because they have aspects that you know you dislike, or you can look into other types of jobs because you know the aspects of something you really enjoy.

Fill in the table below with a few of the job ideas you have in mind. This will help you assess which jobs will suit you best based on various different criteria. You will also be able to see what is needed from you in order to step into these careers.

Job Title	Education and Training	Interests	Skills and Abilities	Growth and Potential Salary

8

SECURING YOUR FUTURE

About 58 million Americans do not have any retirement savings (Beckman, 2023). As a teenager, you probably don't think about retirement all that often. It might seem like something that is very far away and probably something that you don't have to think about. However, retirement creeps up on you pretty quickly. Not only that but starting to save as early as possible is essential to having a good retirement.

When you retire, you don't really have an income because you aren't working. The only way you will be able to live a good life is if you have saved up over the years. There are a lot of expenses when it comes to retirement because, as you get older, you might also become ill and have medical bills to consider. You might also want to live your best life at that point because you do not have to think about work. If you don't have any money, then you'll be stuck in your house or even at an old age home. This is probably not the type of retirement you want, so being able to plan early is a really good idea.

GETTING INSURED

When you become an adult, insurance is essential. It is even more important when you reach retirement age because you might not have time to make money to pay off large bills. Insurance can be thought of as a safety net when it comes to your finances. We all know that unexpected things can happen all the time. You might get into a car accident, or your plumbing system in your house might burst. Perhaps something valuable to you is stolen or, for some reason, your car randomly breaks down. Most people don't think these bad situations can happen to them, but unfortunately, life is unexpected. Sometimes things happen and we don't have control over them. But we are still financially responsible for these things.

An insurance policy makes sure that you are able to afford an emergency if one does happen. This is over and above the money you have saved up for an emergency because these financial responsibilities will probably cost more than anything you can save. For example, if there is a natural disaster and your house is destroyed, you are probably not going to have enough money saved up to fix your house and replace all the items. An insurance policy will help you get the repairs done so you can go back to your original standard of living.

When you take out an insurance policy, you pay a monthly premium and get covered for certain emergencies and unforeseen circumstances. Every insurance policy is different, and that is why you must read the terms and conditions to know what is covered. Some insurance policies are for health, and others are for homes or cars. You might need to get more than one insurance policy to cover the various areas of your life. When you are older and reach retirement age, you might need to increase the amount of insurance you have just so that you can be sure everything is taken care of. The amount you pay for insurance will depend on many things, including your risk factors and previous insurance claims.

It is important to do your research and find out what type of insurance is available. Different insurance providers will have different monthly premiums as well as different benefits. You need to be able to look at your life and decide what is going to be the most important thing. A good thing to look out for with an insurance company is the different types of insurance they offer. If you are able to get all your insurance policies from one provider, you might be able to get a discount. You also need to make sure your insurance provider is reputable, which means they have a higher chance of providing for their customers. If you choose an insurance provider just because it's the cheapest, you might end up choosing one that will not pay out when you go through an emergency. Bigger insurance companies tend to be the most reliable because they have more financial strength and, therefore, are more likely to pay out a huge claim if needed.

It is also a good idea to check out how their customer service is because you will be in contact with their agents. If they are slow to reply or unfriendly, then they could put major stress on you when you are going through an emergency. This is why it's important to call and communicate with any kind of insurance provider before you decide whether or not to go with them.

Even as a teenager, it is important to have insurance because bad things can still happen. Health insurance is essential, and if you have a car, so is car insurance. Car insurance will cover you if you get into a car accident or your car breaks down for some other reason. Health insurance is there if you get sick or are diagnosed with a disease; your insurance can cover your medical bills. Medical bills can be some of the most expensive and can put a lot of financial pressure on you and your parents. If your parents have health insurance, it is most likely that you will fall under their plan. In most cases, you would be able to stay on your parents health insurance plan up until the age of 26, even if you have moved out of the house. This might help you save some money, as plans that include multiple people usually come with discounts. You can ask your parents to stay on their plan and just pay them back for the premium.

If you have a job, you might be able to get health insurance through your employer. If you are just a part-time worker, this might not be possible, but it's always good to check with your employer to see what they offer. Many employers will require you to work at the company for a minimum number of days before they activate your health insurance. Another option is government-funded medical assistance or medical aid. This depends on where you are in the world, so make sure that your government offers this. This is usually only offered to certain people who qualify. That usually means you have to be below a certain income level or have a certain disability. If you are older and working, then you can also get an individual health insurance policy for yourself.

CREATING AN EMERGENCY FUND

Even if you have insurance in all areas of your life, it is still important for you to have an emergency fund. Your insurance is not going to cover every kind of emergency that could possibly happen. If you have a burst tire, it is likely that your insurance might not cover that. You would have to pay for a new tire on your own. Having an emergency fund ready to go is an important part of any kind of financial plan.

Your emergency fund will be a specific amount of money that you keep in a savings account. It can be used for any kind of emergency, regardless of the size, but you shouldn't be using it for things that you want. Your favorite singer coming to town and buying concert tickets is probably not an emergency.

When you have an emergency fund, you don't have to get into debt for unforeseen circumstances. If you don't have any money tucked away and there is a huge financial expense that suddenly comes your way, you'll probably have to take out a loan in order to pay for it. The point of an emergency fund is to have something for a rainy day.

Every person will probably need a different amount in their emergency fund, depending on how much they make and their lifestyle. A good rule of thumb is to have three to six months' worth of expenses saved up in your emergency fund. I would say the closer you can get to six months' worth of expenses, the better. This will also give you some security if you lose your main source of income. Let's say you are laid off or fired from your job. If you have a six-month emergency fund, then you have six months to find a new job. This way, you aren't stressed out about what you're going to do, and you won't take the first job offer just because you're desperate. You have the time to look for a job that is perfect for you.

Now that you know why it is so important for you to have an emergency fund, you need to take the time to actually build it up. If you follow the steps below, you will be able to create and sustain a healthy emergency fund.

Set the Number

The first thing you need to do is set aside the amount you need in your emergency fund. Even as a teenager, it is important to have one, so work out what your expenses every month come to. If you have a budget, all you have to do is look at it to find your number. Then multiply that number by three to six. That is the number that you should be saving toward.

Put It In Your Budget

The next thing you need to do is make sure it is in your budget. This means you should create a plan to reach the goal. Let's say you want $500 in your emergency account. It will probably take you a good few months until you can reach it. If you save $50 for the next 10 months, you'll be able to reach this goal. You can put this in your budget so you can be sure that you are saving $50 each month. Since this is such an important part of a budget, this will be one of the biggest priorities you have.

Once you're done saving for your emergency account, you don't have to have this in your budget anymore. I would suggest that if you have any extra money every now and then, you can put it towards your emergency fund so you can build it up quicker. As soon as you have your goal amount, you don't really have to worry about the emergency fund anymore.

If You Use It, Replace It

There will probably come a time when you have to use the money in your emergency account. That is what it is there for. Once you have used the money, you need to replace it. This means that you will have to put your emergency fund contributions back into your budget.

Building it back up to your goal amount as quickly as possible should be a priority.

Another thing to consider is that as you get older and your expenses increase, you will have to increase the amount in your emergency fund. Once you get your first job or get an increase, you should put more money into the emergency fund. This way, you can always make sure that you have enough money for your current standard of living.

SAVING FOR RETIREMENT

Saving for retirement is really important, but you need to have a plan. This will also help you commit to your plan so you can keep going. We have already spoken about all the different types of retirement accounts you can have. As soon as you get one of these retirement accounts, you can start investing in it.

Start Small

You don't have to pick a huge contribution number from the beginning. It is better that you start small and start early rather than waiting until you have more money in order to invest in your retirement. Even if you are too young to open up a retirement account, you can still create a habit of investing. All you need to do is put a certain amount of money in a savings account. Once you are able to open up your retirement account, you can put that money away there. Once you start earning more money, you can increase the amount.

See if Your Employer Matches Contributions

As mentioned earlier, depending on the type of retirement account you have, your employer might match your contributions. This is usually true if you have a 401(k)-retirement account. If your employer is matching your contributions, make sure you find out how much they are able to match. If you can, you should try to max out these contributions so you can make the most of this benefit. You'll be able to take your 401(k) to a new company if you are moving jobs. However, the benefits might not be the same, so if you are choosing to change jobs, make sure you understand what kind of retirement accounts the new job offers.

Automate It

It can be difficult to remember to put money into your retirement accounts. This is why it's always best to automate it if you can. You can set up an automatic payment for the day after your payday. This way, your money goes out of your account and into your retirement account quickly and easily. You don't even have to think about it, so it makes saving a whole lot easier. This also allows you to prioritize your retirement rather than focusing on other things.

Put Away Extra

There might be a few months out of the year when you have a bit of extra money. Maybe you got a bonus, or it was your birthday, and you got some extra cash. Rather than spending it all on things that are not important, put it away in your retirement accounts. This way, you can benefit from it in the long run. Many people blow all of their bonus money, but they don't spend it on things that are important. You can always use some of your extra money for things that you really want but try to make decisions that are going to benefit you for a longer period of time. When your retirement does come around, you will be so thankful that you prioritized that.

ACTIVITY: LIVING PAYCHECK TO PAYCHECK

Many people live paycheck to paycheck, and it is stressful because you are living right on the limit. First play the game Spent (linked below), then fill out the exercises in this document: **https://shorturl.at/ciJKY**

Spent is a great game where you can go through the motions of someone in debt. You will find some really difficult scenarios and be faced with some tough choices. It teaches you what it is like so you can avoid a negative financial situation in the future. Once you are done playing, take some time to answer the questions found in the Google Doc and write down a few sentences about what you have learned.

ACTIVITY: RETIREMENT QUIZ

Take some time to answer the questions in this retirement quiz. This will help you to be better prepared for retirement and understand what is necessary.

- Michael's grandfather told him that he is going to live off Social Security when he is retired. What exactly is Social Security?
- What is the retirement age in your country or state?
- Sarah's dad says that he wants to retire at the age of 50. Is this allowed?
- Why do you think it is important to save for retirement?

CONCLUSION

When it comes to finances, things can get complicated. Sometimes when adults are talking about financial matters, it can go completely over your head. It just seems like a whole bunch of numbers and stats. Now that you've come to the end of the book, you should understand the basics of finances. Working on your finances isn't just for adults. In fact, when you start earlier, you put yourself in a much better position. Now you have the opportunity to learn and make mistakes when you don't have a lot of financial pressure on you. You can learn comfortably and practice building habits that will benefit you in the long run.

Building up your personal finances is all about building the right habits. Things like budgeting and saving are things that can become second nature to you when you practice. Even if you only earn five dollars a month, you can still budget and save. It's not about how much you earn right now but about learning how to manage what you have.

If you feel like you want more responsibility with your finances, take some time to speak to your parents about this. Tell them why you want this responsibility, and let them know that you are ready for it. If you develop a plan as to how you're going to use your money, this will help you convince them. Then you can start building good financial habits and managing your own finances.

Remember that setting financial goals is incredibly important. This is what's going to guide you in the right direction. Your financial goals might change as you get older, but the habits you have built by working towards them are going to last you forever. You don't have to have everything figured out right now, but as soon as you start setting goals, you can have a clearer vision of how you want your future to look. You can start thinking about what will happen after school and then start planning for it. This way, you can start making better decisions about what you want to study or where your career is going.

You will quickly notice that once you start working on your personal finances, things become a lot easier. It will almost become second nature, but you first must take action. As soon as you take the first few steps, you will have a better idea of your finances. Pick one or two things in this book that you want to implement right now. Then write down a plan for how you are going to implement those things. This is going to be a starting point, and from there, you can move forward into other aspects of your finances. This is how you get the ball rolling and make sure that you are fully prepared for all things finances.

If you have enjoyed reading this book and it has helped you, I would love it if you would leave a review on Amazon or whatever platform you purchased it on. Your feedback is appreciated, and I know that as soon as you start implementing what you have learned, your finances are going to look a whole lot better. You'll be in full control, and that is truly powerful. I wish you all the luck in your upcoming journey and future.

REFERENCES

Adams, R. (2022, March 17). *Best Investments for Teenagers [What to Invest In as a Teen]*. Young and the Invested. https://youngandthein vested.com/best-investments-for-teenagers/

Adams, R. (2022, December 26). *40+ ways to make money as a teenager [fast + smart, 2023]*. Young and the Invested. https://youngandthein vested.com/ways-to-make-money-as-a-teenager/

Adams, R. (2023, January 13). *How to open a bank account for a minor: Steps, what you need*. Young and the Invested. https://youngandthein vested.com/how-to-open-a-bank-account-for-a-minor/

American Century Investments. (2021, February 23). *Financial literacy for teens: Spending wants vs needs*. American Century Investments. https://www.americancentury.com/insights/financial-literacy-teens-spending-wants-needs/

AmeriChoice Federal Credit Union. (2017, August 23). *How to Get Your First Credit Card as a Teenager*. AmeriChoice Federal Credit Union. https://www.americhoice.org/blog/get-first-credit-card-teenager/

Beckman, K. (2023, February 16). *58 million Americans have no retirement savings: How employers can help*. BenefitsPRO. https://www.benefit spro.com/2023/02/16/58m-americans-have-no-retirement-savings-how-employers-can-help/?slreturn=20230505024210

Beers, B. (2023, March 23). *How to open a brokerage account for a child*. Investopedia. https://www.investopedia.com/ask/answers/can-someone-not-yet-legal-age-open-brokerage-account/

Better Money Habits. (n.d.). *Teen guide: 5 steps to saving for something you really want*. Better Money Habits. https://bettermoneyhabits.banko famerica.com/en/saving-budgeting/saving-money-as-a-teenager

Bloomenthal, A. (2019). *Credit Card: What It Is, How It Works, and How to Get One*. Investopedia. https://www.investopedia.com/terms/c/creditcard.asp

Boyles, K. (n.d.). *42 in-demand high-paying trade jobs that don't need a degree*. Snagajob. https://www.snagajob.com/blog/post/42-in-demand-high-paying-trade-jobs-that-dont-need-a-degree

Brennan, C. (2017, May 31). *What are the best credit cards for teens?* Credit Karma. https://www.creditkarma.com/credit-cards/i/credit-cards-for-teens

Brokamp, R. (2023, May 12). *8 Strategies to Save for Retirement*. The Motley Fool. https://www.fool.com/retirement/strategies/

Chase. (n.d.). *Can a teenager open a bank account?* Chase. https://www.chase.com/personal/banking/education/basics/can-a-teenager-open-a-bank-account

Claim Your Future. (n.d.). *About the game*. Claim Your Future. https://fame.claimyourfuture.org/about-the-game/

Coleman, K. (2023, May 19). *25 high-paying jobs that don't require a four-year degree*. Ramsey Solutions. https://www.ramseysolutions.com/career-advice/high-paying-jobs-without-a-degree

Connick, W. (2017, November 2). *Your teenager should have a retirement account. Here's why*. The Motley Fool. https://www.fool.com/retirement/2017/11/02/your-teenager-should-have-a-retirement-account-her.aspx

Consumer Financial Protection Bureau. (n.d.). *An essential guide to building an emergency fund*. Consumer Financial Protection Bureau. https://www.consumerfinance.gov/an-essential-guide-to-building-an-emergency-fund/

Consumer Financial Protection Bureau. (n.d.). *Banking basics card game*. Consumer Financial Protection Bureau. chrome-extension://efaidnbmnnnibpcajpcglclefindmkaj/https://files.consumerfinance.gov/f/documents/cfpb_building_block_activities_banking-basics-card-game_guide.pdf

Copper. (n.d.). *Teen banking: Budgeting for teens*. Copper. https://www.getcopper.com/guide/budgeting

Dowshen, S. (n.d.). *Health insurance basics*. Nemours Children's Health. https://kidshealth.org/en/teens/insurance.html

Doyle, A. (2021, August 19). *How to Get Your First Part-Time Job for Teens*. The Balance. https://www.thebalancemoney.com/tips-for-getting-your-first-part-time-job-2058650

Easy Peasy Finance for Kids and Beginners. (2020, April 4). *What is compound interest? A simple explanation for kids, teens and beginners.* Easy Peasy Finance for Kids and Beginners. https://www.easypeasy finance.com/compound-interest-for-kids-teens/

Easy Peasy Finance. (2021, March 17). *What are taxes? A super simple explanation for kids, teens and beginners.* Easy Peasy Finance. https://www.easypeasyfinance.com/taxes-for-kids-teens-beginners/

Ellis, K. (2022, February 22). *How do student loans work?* Ramsey Solutions. https://www.ramseysolutions.com/debt/how-do-student-loans-work

FamilyEducation. (n.d.). *Teach kids about borrowing money.* FamilyEducation. https://www.familyeducation.com/teens/values-responsibilities/teach-kids-about-borrowing-money

Fay, B. (2012). *Good debt vs. bad debt.* Debt.org. https://www.debt.org/advice/good-vs-bad/

Fernando, J. (2023, April 5). *Return on investment (ROI): How to Calculate It and What It Means.* Investopedia. https://www.investopedia.com/terms/r/returnoninvestment.asp

Geier, B. (2021, February 10). *11 common types of investments and how they work.* SmartAsset. https://smartasset.com/investing/types-of-investment

Get Schooled. (2023, May 18). *Everything teens should know about building credit.* Get Schooled. https://getschooled.com/article/5787-teens-and-credit-scores/

Gobler, E. (2022, June 2). *Investing for teens: Everything you need to know.* The Balance. https://www.thebalancemoney.com/investing-guide-for-teens-and-parents-4588018

Grange Insurance. (n.d.). *What is insurance and why is it important?* Grange Insurance. https://www.grangeinsurance.com/tips/what-is-insurance-why-is-it-important

Greenlight. (n.d.). *How to make money as a teen — 20 ideas to get started.* Greenlight. https://greenlight.com/blog/how-to-make-money-as-a-teen-20-ideas-to-get-started

Grossman, A. (2019, November 25). *12 fun budgeting activities pdfs for students (kids & teens).* Money Prodigy. https://www.moneyprodigy.

com/fun-budgeting-activities-pdfs/

Grossman, A. L. (2021, March 8). *Short-Term financial goals for high school students (26 examples)*. Money Prodigy. https://www.moneyprodigy.com/short-term-financial-goals-for-high-school-students/

Hayes, A. (2023, March 16). *Entrepreneur: What it means to be one and how to get started*. Investopedia. https://www.investopedia.com/terms/e/entrepreneur.asp

Housman, D. (2020, August 13). *Millions of Millennials Spend More on Coffee (and Other Things) than Retirement*. The Simple Dollar. https://www.thesimpledollar.com/save-money/millions-of-millennials-spend-more-on-coffee-and-other-things-than-retirement/?utm_source=feedburner&utm_medium=feed&utm_campaign=Feed%3A+thesimpledollar+%28The+Simple+Dollar%29

Huffman, M. (2019, December 19). *How to teach kids and teens about debt*. Alliant. https://www.alliantcreditunion.org/money-mentor/how-to-teach-kids-and-teens-about-debt

Indeed. (2022, September 5). *8 reasons why learning a trade skill is a good idea*. Indeed. https://ca.indeed.com/career-advice/resumes-cover-letters/trade-skill

Investor.gov. (n.d.). *Compound interest calculator*. Investor.gov. https://www.investor.gov/financial-tools-calculators/calculators/compound-interest-calculator

Irby, L. (2022, July 5). *How can Teenagers Build Credit?* The Balance. https://www.thebalancemoney.com/help-your-child-build-a-good-credit-score-960520

Kneil, L. (2018, October 31). *Can you succeed without college? Yes, but it's complicated*. Northeastern University: Bachelor's Degree Completion. https://bachelors-completion.northeastern.edu/news/succeeding-without-college/

Kollmeyer, B. (n.d.). *How these teens are having fun in today's stock market, and, for the most part, making money*. MarketWatch. https://www.marketwatch.com/story/these-teens-are-having-fun-in-todays-stock-market-they-share-the-secrets-to-their-success-11615218810

Lake, R. (2023, March 3). *Teens and income taxes.* Investopedia. https://www.investopedia.com/teens-and-income-taxes-7152618

Laming, D. (2023, June 19). *8 Reasons Learning a Trade Is the Best Career Choice You Can Make.* Tradesman Saver. https://www.tradesman saver.co.uk/tradesman-insights/8-reasons-learning-trade-is-best-career-choice-can-make/

Lobell, K. O. (2020, October 15). *Money foundations for kids: Compound interest.* MoneyGeek. https://www.moneygeek.com/financial-plan ning/compound-interest-for-kids/

LogoLife. (2022, October 6). *How to get started as a teen entrepreneur.* LogoLife. https://logolife.org/how-to-get-started-as-a-teen-entrepreneur/

Martin, A. (2022, September 12). *6 ways to get out of debt.* Bankrate. https://www.bankrate.com/personal-finance/debt/ways-to-get-out-of-debt/

Merrill Edge. (2018). *10 ways to help you boost your retirement savings — whatever your age.* Merrill Edge. https://www.merrilledge.com/arti cle/10-tips-to-help-you-boost-your-retirement-savings-whatever-your-age-ose

Mint. (2020, August 17). *50/30/20 budgeting rule: How to use it [instruc-tions + calculator].* MintLife Blog. https://mint.intuit.com/blog/saving/how-to-budget/

Mint. (2020, November 2). *Zero-Based budgeting: The ultimate guide.* MintLife Blog. https://mint.intuit.com/blog/budgeting/zero-based-budgeting/

Mint. (2022, June 30). *Budgeting for teens: 14 tips for growing your money young.* MintLife Blog. https://mint.intuit.com/blog/budgeting/budgeting-for-teens/

Mitra, M. (2020, November 23). *Meet the teens saving for retirement.* Money. https://money.com/teenagers-retirement-savings-roth-ira/

Muller, C. (2022, October 11). *How to spend money wisely---a guide for teens.* Moneyunder30. https://www.moneyunder30.com/how-to-spend-money-wisely-for-teens

Muller, C. (2023, March 27). *Banking 101---A guide for teenagers (and*

anyone who needs A refresher). Money under 30. https://www.
moneyunder30.com/banking-basics

Neidel, C. (2019, December 17). *Needs vs. wants: How to budget for both.*
NerdWallet. https://www.nerdwallet.com/article/finance/finan
cial-needs-versus-wants

Next Gen Personal Finance. (n.d.). *Who will pitch it to win it?* Google
Docs. https://docs.google.com/document/d/1T-
s3qOYODvFLHu5V0HBZM7WowZS91OslDVwWieB_h0c/edit

Next Gen Personal Finance. (n.d.). *INTERACTIVE: Living paycheck to
paycheck.* Google Docs. https://docs.google.com/document/d/
1phvcH9Ln_UOPjX_W32gU6dfKxFfJVCxzvdsT_f7C_U0/edit

Next Gen Personal Finance. (n.d.). *INTERACTIVE: Which jobs align with
my interests?* Google Docs. https://docs.google.com/document/d/
1dHJHHQ1dJY1-OIE9B7YEKszELE4PDrB1p56pB6J1DGQ/edit

Next Gen Personal Finance. (n.d.). *MATH: Return on investment.* Google
Docs. https://docs.google.com/document/d/1fGgi7u0ef5mxZ-y-
vaEeSwHqugHaLuk4rtE2aAM4S14/edit#

Next Gen Personal Finance. (n.d.). *READ: Retirement Basics.* Google
Docs. Retrieved June 9, 2023, from https://docs.google.com/docu
ment/d/
101BvWF0xpvd7m893beiMmlqrRCX3ti7JdqRt65y4OAY/edit

Next Gen Personal Finance. (2019, July 15). *INTERACTIVE: FICO credit
scores.* Google Docs. https://docs.google.com/document/d/1hkzZrc
doKIeubycSwxR-U965Q3GFjMHf8MnMRdAoI7A/edit

Next Gen Personal Finance. (2020, March 18). *CALCULATE: Shopping
with interest.* Google Docs. https://docs.google.com/document/d/
1MdA4T2PY-qLuIW_B_lq2KoKv39XwKDd7m0zOCsnA2gU/
edit#heading=h.1tvb1m6yciuq

Next Gen Personal Finance. (2023, April 9). *Question: $1,000,000 or a
penny that 2x every day for 30 days?* Next Gen Personal Finance.
https://www.ngpf.org/blog/question-of-the-day/question-of-the-
day-would-you-rather-have-1000000-or-start-with-a-penny-and-
double-your-money-every-day-for-30-days2021/

O'Neill, B. (2016, November). *The 30-day $100 savings challenge.* Rutgers
New Jersey Agricultural Experiment Station. https://njaes.rutgers.

edu/sshw/message/message.php?p=Finance&m=337

O'Shea, A. (2023, June 2). *Investing for kids: How to open a brokerage account for your child*. NerdWallet. https://www.nerdwallet.com/article/investing/set-kids-brokerage-account

Oh, H. (2022, August 9). *Everything you need to know about credit cards for teens*. Seventeen. https://www.seventeen.com/life/school/g40657451/credit-cards-for-teens/

Ownr. (2022, April 13). *40 best small business ideas for teens in 2023*. Ownr. https://www.ownr.co/blog/small-business-ideas-for-teens/

Oxford Royale Academy. (2020, October 20). *14 teen entrepreneurs and how they succeeded*. Oxford Royale Academy. https://www.oxford-royale.com/articles/14-teen-entrepreneurs/

Porter, K. (2021, February 3). *Average American debt statistics*. Bankrate. https://www.bankrate.com/personal-finance/debt/average-american-debt/

Priest, B. (2023, March 3). *How to start saving for retirement in your teens and 20s*. Slavic401k. https://slavic401k.com/how-to-start-saving-for-retirement-in-your-teens-and-20s/

Probasco, J. (2023, April 21). *How to file your child's first income tax return*. Investopedia. https://www.investopedia.com/articles/taxes/08/kids-first-income-tax-return.asp

Push, A. (2023, May 27). *What are the different types of credit scores?* LendingTree. https://www.lendingtree.com/credit-repair/what-are-the-different-types-of-credit-scores/

Quote Investigator. (2011, April 7). *A banker lends you his umbrella when it's sunny and wants it back when it rains*. Quote Investigator. https://quoteinvestigator.com/2011/04/07/banker-umbrella/

Richmond, S. (2019). *Why save for retirement in your 20s?* Investopedia. https://www.investopedia.com/articles/personal-finance/040315/why-save-retirement-your-20s.asp

Rockwood, K. (2020a, September 25). *Banking 101: Understanding how banking works*. Step. https://step.com/money-101/post/a-teens-guide-to-banking

Rockwood, K. (2020b, September 25). *Tracking your finances: A guide for teens*. Step. https://step.com/money-101/post/tracking-your-finances-a-guide-for-teens

Rosenburg, A. (2021). *15 ways to get a job as a teen*. WikiHow. https://www.wikihow.com/Get-a-Job-As-a-Teen

Safier, R. (2022, May 31). *7 ways to pay back your student loans faster as an international student*. Mpower Financing. https://www.mpowerfinancing.com/blog/7-ways-to-repay-your-student-loans-faster

Sagevest Kids. (2016, June 9). *Borrowing*. Sagevest Kids. https://www.kidsfinancialeducation.com/explore-topics/borrowing/

Schwahn, L. (2020, December 18). *What is a budget?* NerdWallet. https://www.nerdwallet.com/article/finance/what-is-a-budget

Securian Financial. (n.d.). *5 steps to build an emergency fund*. Securian Financial. https://www.securian.com/insights-tools/articles/5-steps-to-building-an-emergency-fund.html

Shell, A. (2020, March 17). *Get motivated to eliminate debt*. AARP. https://www.aarp.org/money/credit-loans-debt/info-2020/two-ways-to-pay-off-debt.html

Shook, J. (2022, September 2). *Fall into a new career: The benefits of learning a skilled trade*. Southern Careers Institute. https://scitexas.edu/blog/fall-into-a-new-career-the-benefits-of-learning-a-skilled-trade/

Sleight, M. (2023, February 8). *How to find the best life insurance policy for a teenager*. MoneyGeek. https://www.moneygeek.com/insurance/life/best-for-teenagers/

Smith, L. (2023, February 12). *Good debt vs. bad debt: The differences*. Investopedia. https://www.investopedia.com/articles/pf/12/good-debt-bad-debt.asp

SOCU. (n.d.). *What does it mean to be a smart spender?* SOCU. https://www.socu.com/blog/teen-smart-spending

Vamdatt, R. (2020, October 30). *What is investing? A simple explanation for kids, teens & beginners*. Easy Peasy Finance for Kids and Beginners. https://www.easypeasyfinance.com/investing-for-kids-financial-literacy/

Warner, A. (2022, May 19). *5 reasons to consider community college*. USN. https://www.usnews.com/education/community-colleges/articles/reasons-to-consider-community-college

Warren, K. (2023, May 3). *Credit tips for teens*. Investopedia. https://www.investopedia.com/credit-tips-for-teens-7152864

White, A. (2020, January 13). *Alaskans carry the highest credit card balance —here's the average credit card balance in every state*. CNBC. https://www.cnbc.com/select/average-credit-card-balance-by-state/

Young Adult Money. (2020, November 6). *6 different ways to budget your money*. Young Adult Money. https://www.youngadultmoney.com/6-different-ways-to-budget-your-money/

Youth Villages. (2021, September 20). *Achieving goals - Ayla's story*. Youth Villages. https://youthvillages.org/achieving-goals-aylas-story/

www.ingramcontent.com/pod-product-compliance
Lightning Source LLC
Chambersburg PA
CBHW031530120626
46545CB00005B/2086